BUILDING A FAMILY WITH OPTIMUM CHILD REARING

BUILDING A FAMILY WITH OPTIMUM CHILD REARING

A Guide for Teachers, Caregivers, Counselors, and Advisers in the Era of Globalization

Noel Julius Ntawigaya

FOREWORD BY
Tuli Kassimoto

RESOURCE *Publications* · Eugene, Oregon

BUILDING A FAMILY WITH OPTIMUM CHILD REARING
A Guide for Teachers, Caregivers, Counselors, and Advisers in the Era of
Globalization

Resource Publications
An Imprint of Wipf and Stock Publishers
199 W. 8th Ave., Suite 3
Eugene, OR 97401

www.wipfandstock.com

PAPERBACK ISBN: 979-8-3852-2068-7
HARDCOVER ISBN: 979-8-3852-2069-4
EBOOK ISBN: 979-8-3852-2070-0

I dedicate this book to my children, Lilian, Vicky, Prosper, and Deborah, as the principles expounded in this book begin to take root in their lives. I advise them to embrace and live by the values of optimal upbringing. May they grow to become exemplary parents in their own families, contributing positively to the communities they inhabit and, ultimately, to the nation as a whole.

Table of Contents

Foreword

TANZANIA LIKE OTHER COUNTRIES in the southern Sahara region and the rest of world, is undergoing a pivotal period of transformation across economic, social, cultural, and political landscapes. These changes have permeated every aspect of society to varying extents, with the upbringing and growth of children being particularly affected. The upbringing of today's children demands a heightened level of attention and a profound understanding of various issues. This is because, alongside improvements in healthcare services, there exist contracts, laws, institutions, and numerous guidelines that safeguard and advocate for the rights of the child. Furthermore, children's awareness of various issues related to rights, responsibilities, and diverse opportunities has multiplied exponentially in recent years. It is within this context that the book on family and upbringing in the era of globalization has been presented at a timely juncture.

This book meticulously analyzes the concept of family from various perspectives, child upbringing and development, theories of upbringing, types of families, styles of upbringing, and the current environment of upbringing in these times of globalization. This book serves as a well of knowledge for teachers, parents, caregivers, counselors, and advisers across the globe.

Currently, the upbringing and growth of children require a broad understanding of various aspects, including changes in brain development, emotions, the body, and the environments that surround children. Scientific and technological advancements have facilitated communication, improved healthcare services, and increased interaction among people, expertise, and cultures. Despite the benefits, these changes come with challenges, particularly in the realm of child-rearing and development.

For early childhood educators and teachers in the early grades of primary education, this book will aid in understanding children, their growth, and their learning processes. This includes recognizing children with special needs, such as those with accelerated or delayed understanding, discovering various talents in children, and fostering self-awareness, as well as building relationships with the families from which the children come.

The author has thoroughly and comprehensively discussed these matters to assist teachers in enhancing child upbringing, teaching, and learning. It is crucial to remember that in all aspects of life, today's success is built on foundations laid yesterday and the day before.

This book will be immensely helpful for parents and caregivers in understanding the physical, emotional, intellectual, and behavioral aspects of a child's upbringing and development. It provides techniques and strategies on creating a home environment that will help prepare the child to become a well-rounded individual with contributions to their personal life, family, and the nation at large.

Considering the context of Tanzania as an example, the concept of guidance and counseling is not new in the society and culture. For instance, our elders have traditionally shared advice and counsel on various aspects of life. Considering that the foundation for a child's development is laid from a young age, this book will be a significant aid for advisers and counselors. It opens doors to understanding the environment of upbringing and growth of Tanzanian children by integrating various theories of upbringing, family, and the realities we experience in our daily lives. Having reflected the context of Tanzanian society and culture, this book is also helpful to other societies apart from Tanzania depending on the historical nature of their culture.

It is my hope that this book has opened a platform for discussions on the most effective and appropriate ways to nurture and raise Tanzanian children and those from the rest of the world who will find the contents of the book more helpful with an independent, globally oriented perspective aimed at solving their societal challenges within the Tanzanian context and the outside context.

Tuli Kassimoto
Associate Professor (Educational Foundations) and
Deputy Vice Chancellor (Academic Affairs) - Teofilo Kisanji University,
MBEYA – TANZANIA.

Acknowledgements

IN EVERY SUCCESS a human achieves, it is an undeniable truth that the primary assistance comes from divine empowerment. In writing this book, God has been my foremost help, as the knowledge, strength, and health that enabled me to write this book have been given by Him. Therefore, I give Him all the praise and honor for enabling me to write this book.

It is my belief that, all living beings depend on each other. This sentence forms the foundation for expressing gratitude to all individuals who, in various ways, have ultimately contributed to the success of this book, which is now ready to serve its intended audience. The acknowledgments go to Prof. Elia Mligo for mentoring me on how to write books, enabling me to write this important book. Additionally, I am truly grateful to Dr. Laurent Gabriel Ndijuye, an expert in early childhood education and child upbringing from the University of Dodoma, for reading this book and providing significant inputs. Moreover, I extend my heartfelt thanks to Prof. Tuli Kassimoto for reading this book and writing a brilliant foreword. Lastly, I want to express my deepest thanks to my family, my wife, and my children for their cooperation throughout the entire writing process of this book. At times, they wished to be closer to me, but I missed their presence due to the demands of writing this book. Nevertheless, they displayed patience and understanding, and for that, I am extremely grateful.

List of Acronyms

BAKITA - Baraza la Kiswahili la Taifa (National Kiswahili Council)
BAKIZA - Baraza la Kiswahili la Zanzibar
        (Zanzibar Kiswahili Council)
CHS - Commission for Human Security
IDCFS - Illinois Department of Children and Family Services
JMT - Jamhuri ya Muungano wa Tanzania (United Republic of
        Tanzania)
PACESH - Shinyanga Paralegal Aid Centre
TV - Televisheni (Television)
UNHCR - United Nations High Commissioner for Refugees
UNWTO - United Nations World Tourism Organization
UPE - Universal Primary Education
WHO - World Health Organization

Introduction

THE BASIS OF THE BOOK

THE HISTORY AND EXPERIENCES a person gains in life serve as assets and opportunities to educate the society they live in, provided that these opportunities are utilized appropriately. Therefore, the experiences that the author, as a teacher, counselor, and advisor to students across various levels and educational settings, have been the source of inspiration for this book. Drawing from this wealth of experience, the author, in roles such as a teacher, counselor, and advisor over an extended period, witnessed various behaviors, both positive and negative, exhibited by students. These behaviors were influenced by the systems and styles of upbringing they received from their families.

The author firmly believes in the significant differences in parenting styles among different families, both historically and up to the present. The book therefore, aims to be a valuable source of knowledge and guidance for those involved in the upbringing and development of children. The intention is to educate the community on the importance of effective parenting and provide insights into various parenting perspectives that contribute to the positive development of children.

CONTEXT OF THE BOOK

In today's world, society comprises different generations, including the fading old generation, the thriving intermediate generation, and the modern generation, which consists predominantly of children and youth. These generations are interdependent, and each is influenced by the behaviors and systems of the preceding generations.

Significant changes have been observed in the ethics of children and youth in recent years. These changes are largely attributed to various parenting systems at the levels of family, community, and the nation as a whole. Additionally, Rwegelera informs that these cultural flows are associated with the expanding scope of globalization, predominantly influenced by Western and American interests.[1] The difference between one generation and another lies in the styles of parenting provided between generations. Therefore, the strengths and weaknesses of any generation are interpreted based on the parenting practices being implemented and observed by the respective generation.

The present generation, which is significantly influenced by a lifestyle that embraces globalization, should be nurtured on ethical foundations in accordance with the traditions, customs, and cultural heritage of our society. For instance, in the past, each community in Tanzania had its own system of upbringing children and youth, guided by the traditions and customs of that specific community. Some ethnic groups had practices like "JANDO" the rite for boys and "UNYAGO" the rite for girls. In these rites of passage, many aspects of life focusing on fostering good values for the community were taught. For example, issues of maturity, responsibility to the family and society, as well as the aspects of married life and independence were covered. These teachings contributed to building a society that knows its responsibilities while adhering to its ethical values.

However, this traditional system of upbringing, despite its merits and demerits, has continued to disappear due to the impact

---

1. Rwegelera, *The Effect of Globalization*, 157.

of the current lifestyle, which is largely built on the foundations of globalization. Many parents and guardians have forgotten the foundations of good upbringing in line with the traditions and customs of their communities. Instead, they have totally adopted a system of parenting that reflects globalization, leading to a generation with values contrary to their traditions and customs.

Therefore, it is my belief that this book, to a large extent, will help in building a solid foundation for the proper upbringing of a child and ultimately contribute to having better families, especially in these times of globalization where violence against children and poor upbringing of children with high erosion of ethical values seem to be increasing.

Since this book has been written basing on the context of Tanzania where the National language is Kiswahili, some information has been cited and translated directly from different sources written in Kiswahili language as it indicates in the bibliography.

INTENDED AUDIENCE

The intended audience of this book includes professionals in counseling and guidance, especially in the context of child rearing in the era of globalization. Additionally, the book will be a valuable resource for parents, guardians, school teachers, marriage counselors, family and parenting workshop facilitators, and all stakeholders involved in matters of child upbringing and protection. The contents of this book can be enjoyed by anybody all over the world because the issue of child rearing is a global phenomenon. By reading this book, the author hopes that all target readers will benefit and, in turn, become pillars in helping to build strong, responsible and ethical families and communities that can analyze good and bad rearing, especially in these times of globalization.

CHAPTER 1

The Theory of Family

INTRODUCTION

ACCORDING TO JACOBSEN, FURSMAN, Bryant, Claridge and Jensen, the origin and meaning of the word 'family' can be interpreted from various perspectives such as anthropological, sociological, psychological, economic, and biological, depending on an individual's or a group's viewpoint.[1] Since a person's perspective is the result of their independent thoughts on a particular matter, the author of this book interprets the term family in two perspectives:

i. Religious Perspective

ii. Secular Perspective

The differences in these two theories about the family are discussed in more detail below.

---

1. Jacobsen, Fursman, Bryant, Claridge & Jensen, *Theories of Family and Policy*, 18–57.

RELIGIOUS PERSPECTIVE

In the religious perspective, the origin of the term family is derived from the Almighty God as described in the holy books of God (the Bible and the Qur'an). God, when He created the heavens and the earth and created the first human known as Adam and Eve, and commanded them to multiply, giving them the ability to live and rule over all resources, that's when the family began. The Holy Scriptures in the Bible state: "*26 Then God said, 'Let us make mankind in our image, in our likeness, so that they may rule over the fish in the sea and the birds in the sky, over the livestock and all the wild animals, and over all the creatures that move along the ground.' 27 So God created mankind in his own image, in the image of God he created them; male and female he created them. 28 God blessed them and said to them, 'Be fruitful and increase in number; fill the earth and subdue it. Rule over the fish in the sea and the birds in the sky and over every living creature that moves on the ground.'" (Gen, chapter 1, verse 26–28).* From the Holy Bible quotation, it is evident that before this creation, there is no book that shows the existence of human life on the face of the earth.

Thus, it is clear that the origin of the term family comes from the Almighty God in His creation. Therefore, the very first family is the one established by God, consisting of a husband (Adam) and a wife (Eve). From this husband and wife family, various families multiplied. This type of family, originating from God, was built on the foundations of ethical upbringing that respected God by adhering to His guidance. The generation that emerged from this family was responsible for ethical and just upbringing, following the laws of God. The image of good and ethical humanity (family) of today was built by this first generation.

SECULAR PERSPECTIVE

In the Sociological perspective, Mwanahiza explains that a family is a union of a father, mother, children, and close relatives.[2] In the

---

2. Mwanahiza, *Utandawazi na Malezi*, para. 7.

secular perspective, the meaning of the term family is interpreted based on the cultures and societies of people in their earthly environments. In this context, the term family can be interpreted as a group of people living together, such as a father, mother, and children, based on the principle of reproduction. This group often forms part of a larger extended family connecting people with a common ancestry (lineage). This type of family is found in all human societies worldwide. Additionally, in an informal sense, Chudhuri describe family as a group of people making up a household (domestic group) who share living and food facilities together.[3] Chudhuri goes further to define the family as an institution or a small community with characteristics of communal living, shared economy, and collaborative production with an institutional structure that has laws, traditions, and customs guiding family members to self-identify.[4]

According to the perspective built in this theory, it is evident that the family was established by the Almighty God Himself when the holy books describe that a man (Adam) was created, and then a woman (Eve), who multiplied and eventually formed a family. However, the holy books do not explain the origin of God, meaning His parents, family lineage, and His native land, which opens up room for debate about the reality of His existence and the truth about His creation. The lack of details showing the origin of God and His generation may be the major weakness of this religious theory about the family, as the author highlights in this book.

This type of family built from the secular perspective has a significant responsibility to perpetuate its generation based on the traditions and customs instituted by the forefathers. Therefore, the issue of upbringing children and youth in this type of family depends on the traditions and customs set by the founders of that generation. In this context, these upbringing practices may be influenced by various surrounding environments within that society. Undoubtedly, these differences in traditions and customs

3. Chudhuri, *Social Development and Family*, 3.
4. Ibid. 3.

regarding upbringing contribute to the diversity of behaviors, with some being considered good and others bad.

However, unlike the religious perspective discussed in this chapter, this secular perspective on family does not explicitly indicate the origin of the first family members, namely, father and mother, as described in the religious theory that the first human was created by God. The lack of clear information about the origin of the first family members might be considered a weakness of this theory.

CONCLUSION

In this chapter, the author has illustrated how the theory of family is constructed and historically explained. Despite the differences between the two theories on family, as discussed in this chapter, both perspectives generally emphasize that the family is the crucial institution for the proper upbringing of children and youth worldwide. Therefore, based on the discourse presented in this chapter regarding the family theory from both perspectives, it is evident that the family should nurture the child as a child by providing all the rights of childhood upbringing, preparing them for future adulthood, and as a potential responsible parent in the future.

DISCUSSION QUESTION

Explain how the religious perspective is similar to and different from the secular perspective regarding the concept of family.

CHAPTER 2

Philosophy and Values of Family

INTRODUCTION

IN ORDER FOR A family to thrive, it is essential to examine the elements it should possess and live by. These elements, in one way or another, are philosophy and values of the family. Alongside the family values, a family must also focus on the general responsibilities of the family, as these are the criteria that determine whether a particular family is alive or dead. These responsibilities are detailed and discussed extensively in the next chapter. This situation arises from the fact that what can define an individual is what they believe in and how they fulfill their duties. Additionally, the well-being of an individual or an institution lies in its responsibilities. This chapter defines the concepts of philosophy and values of the family.

There is a significant relationship between philosophy and values. These terms can be likened to what an individual believes (philosophy) and how they live (actions). Due to the connection between these two terms, it can be said that values are fundamentally based on philosophy. Therefore, before discussing family values, it is important to first ask the question: What does the philosophy of family mean?

The term 'philosophy' has been defined in various perspectives. For example, BAKIZA translates philosophy as a branch of education that deals with the nature, meaning, and reasons for things or an individual's perspective on something.[1] Mlaga describes the term philosophy as efforts arising from an individual's abilities with the goal of promoting the establishment of new thoughts, claims of truth related to the nature of our beliefs. This includes evaluating, reviewing, and even discarding outdated beliefs, thus introducing new thoughts that have the potential to be true.[2]

Based on the interpretations provided by BAKIZA and Mlaga, the term philosophy can be translated as a perspective used as a guide for the behavior or conduct of an individual or a group in life. Philosophy is the belief that an individual hold, shaping whether they do or do not do certain things in their daily life. It was also agreed by Nickell and Dorsey that everyone has their philosophy in life, even if they are unaware that they are living by it. They assert that some people and families develop their own philosophies based on their daily experiences and the knowledge that grows as part of life and the challenges they face. Others receive and live by philosophies built by the traditions and customs of their societies[3].

From these explanations, it is evident that philosophy is a belief that grows and solidifies based on the experiences an individual or a group undergoes in their daily lives. Experience is an indispensable factor in life; instead of being dismissed, it should be considered as events that need to be integrated and treated as valuable fabric in life. In our families, experience stands between individuals, acting as a pillar or among family members, involving common interests and activities that enable them to live together, such as entertainment, character, family resource management, and joint participation in education.

---

1. BAKIZA, *Kamusi Fasaha ya Kiswahili*, 80.

2. Mlaga, *Euphrase Kezilahabi*, 1.

3. Nickell & Dorsey, *"Management in Family Living"*, 37. cf. Krone, *"A Personal Philosophy"*, 71.

Philosophy is crucial in a family because the family's philosophy is the only belief that shapes the lives, thoughts, emotions, and overall experience of all family members. The family's philosophy is what builds strong family relationships, family priorities, family interests, and family activities such as choosing a specific job or profession as a family priority. This is where we find that some families prefer a certain job or profession as part of their family philosophy. Therefore, a family without a philosophy lacks a specific direction in its daily activities, especially in nurturing its future generations. This is akin to saying that a family without a philosophy is like a car in motion without front and rear lights. The outcome of driving such a car is collision, either from behind or in front. As mentioned earlier, it is clear that the family's philosophy is confirmed through actions, where if it logically changes in actions, it is referred to as the values of the family.

The term 'value' can be interpreted in various ways. For example, BAKITA translates the word 'value' as something given to a person as a gift, a sign of love, or recognition of work done; something rare or scarce.[4] In this context, the term 'value' in this book means the principles or things that provide a real picture in the actions of a family, group, society, or a specific nation. Values are the things that have been interpreted based on the philosophy of the family, group, society, or nation and are placed into action as their pillars. These are the things that differentiate one family, group, society, or nation from another. Duh and Belak explain that the family system creates specific foundations or values that can be seen and used to set the visions, mission, and goals of the family as an institution.[5] It was further explained that in any society, values are the ones that build the internal intellectual foundations for the members to show what they like and dislike.[6] In any institution, including the family, values form the basis of identity for the members, enable the stability of social systems, guide the leaders of the institution in looking at important matters, guide the leaders of

4. BAKITA, *Kamusi Kuu ya Kiswahili*, 1058.

5. Duh & Belak, *Core Values and Culture*, 50.

6. *Ibid.* 50.

the institution in making crucial decisions, and even facilitate sincere intentions in doing things that are in the interest of the entire institution and not just the personal interests of the institution's leaders.[7] Guertin explains that Family values involve all the ideas of how you want to live your family life, and they are often passed down from previous generations. They can help define behavior in various situations, help youth make good choices, and solidify the bond that your family has. In his explanation, he states that while every family may have a set of values or principles, there are various types of values or principles that seem to overlap, and the specific values of one family or another are based on various values, especially social, political, religious, work-related, ethical, and recreational values. [8] These general values, as listed, are what build the specific values and principles of a family, society, or any nation.

In this book, there are specific values that seem to carry other values and appear to be as important as they can be thought of by any family, society, or nation. Some of these values relate to mutual respect, transparency, accountability, conflict resolution, integrity, patriotism, self-confidence, faith in religion, and family resource management. I can say that values should be the words left for the next generation, and this should be the legacy for the family generation.

MUTUAL RESPECT

This value is a crucial pillar in building a strong family, society, and nation as a whole. According to this book, the term "mutual respect" focuses on the word 'value,' which, according to Mohamed and Mohamed, means to respect, esteem, glorify, submit, care for, follow, obey, honor, praise, or commend.[9] From this interpretation, undoubtedly, when someone talks about mutual respect, they may also mean equal rights, unity, solidarity, love, or

---

7. Deal & Kennedy, *Corporate Cultures.*

8. Guertin, *List of Family Values,* 1.

9. Mohamed & Mohamed, *Kamusi ya Visawe,* 223.

consideration. Here, we are discussing seeing another person in a high state of value, equal to or even higher than oneself. No human is better than others; every human is better for one another. Thus, no human is perfect compared to others; we all have short-comings that we should acknowledge in each other. If anyone sees themselves as superior and without flaws compared to others, they do not possess the qualities of being human. The truth is that the value of a human being is in such balance that we all have an equal right to love or be loved, respect or be respected, and understand or be understood in our imperfections.

According to Jamhuri ya Muungano wa Tanzania (United Republic of Tanzania), all humans are born equal, and everyone deserves the respect of recognizing and appreciating their humanity by their fellow humans.[10] Differences in color, education, income, or leadership positions do not make us less valuable as humans; instead, they show that each person is valuable to another based on the role, status, or respect they have. If we foster a culture of mutual respect (caring for one another, equal rights, unity, solidarity, love, respect, and consideration) in the family, the society we live in will be better, and the nation as a whole will benefit. In this way, mutual respect becomes the foundation of brotherhood within the family because a family that can uphold this value becomes better and has a greater chance of professionally nurturing its future generations. Parents should establish this foundation of mutual respect for their children for the good future of their current and future lives. This is equivalent to saying that in every family gathering, it is crucial to emphasize to the children this behavior and culture of mutual respect.

If children are taught mutual respect, they will love each other, support one another, tolerate each other's weaknesses, respect each other, care for each other within the family, and eventually, this will become their behavior even with people outside their family. This will help eliminate the lack of humanity and cruelty at the family level and subsequently in society at large, ultimately leading to a community free from any form of violence.

10. Jamhuri ya Muungano wa Tanzania, *Katiba ya Tanzania 1977*, 26.

TRANSPARENCY

The term 'transparency' has been interpreted in various perspectives; for example, BAKITA defines transparency as the condition or behavior of speaking without concealing anything.[11] Thus, based on BAKITA's interpretation, transparency appears to be one of the crucial values in families, especially in the current era where society experiences extensive interactions. Due to people's busy schedules, close relationships within many families are decreasing day by day, especially in this age of globalization. Visiting and getting to know each other among family members are diminishing, and instead, people communicate through phone calls and various social media platforms such as email, Facebook, Twitter, Instagram, etc.

Many parents lack sufficient time to sit down with their children to discuss the family's history and various family matters that could help children understand many aspects of their families. The lack of transparency in some families has led many young people to unknowingly marry their relatives. Some end up marrying their sisters, while others marry their brothers from families believed to be distant relatives. Transparency experts, Doughty, Reed and Magrath argue that transparency describes openness, accessibility and public understanding of the family justice system.[12] In my view, transparency is closely related to freedom, the quality of our relationships, the quality of our lives, and the growth of our communities. Hence, our lives can be built or destroyed by the foundation of transparency in our communities.

Listen to this true story from one of my students from a certain region in Tanzania.

There was a single female parent who, in her youth as a young woman, had relationships with two different men from two different regions. These men were traders with varying income

11. BAKITA, *Kamusi Kuu ya Kiswahili*, 1181.

12. Doughty, Reed & Magrath, *Transparency in the Family*.

levels. During her relationships with these two men, the woman found herself pregnant. The pregnancy belonged to the first man she was in a relationship with, who essentially had less money compared to the second man. After discovering that she was pregnant with the child of the first man, she used romantic influence and ended up being involved with the second man, who had more money than the one who impregnated her. A few days before the pregnancy could be identified as belonging to either of the two men, she made non-transparent and untruthful decisions and told the wealthy man, "I am pregnant with your child". Following this, the wealthy man thought it was best to take her as his wife, anticipating the birth of their child. Surprisingly, this wealthy man already had another wife with whom he lived and had older daughters and sons.

Therefore, this woman unknowingly became the second wife and was not aware of it. When she arrived at the home of the wealthy man, she discovered that she was the second wife and had to be submissive since her conscience accused her of not being transparent and truthful about the pregnancy. Later, she lost contact with the first man, and life continued with the wealthy man, who continued to father children with her.

The child born from the first pregnancy was a boy and, during his upbringing, showed exceptional intelligence compared to all the wealthy man's male children, especially those born to his first wife. The wealthy man loved this young man dearly, provided him with a good education in an English-oriented school, and after completing primary education, entrusted him with the responsibility of managing his projects. Between these two, the child and the father, no one knew the secret of their relationship except the young man's mother.

Many years later, when the young man started Form One as an adult due to spending a long time in the management of his father's projects, his mother, due to an unpleasant relationship with the wealthy man, decided to call him and instruct him to go to the region where his biological father lived, whom he had never seen or known beyond the wealthy man. The mother and the young man had already contacted the old man who had given her the pregnancy and who, by that time, had become impoverished and destitute.

When the young man met the man who was his biological father, he felt a resemblance but faced difficult circumstances. Blood is thicker than water. The young man felt something; his heart hurt, especially regarding the life of the old man. They spoke, but the old man did not tell him that he was his father, and the young man did not ask him anything about their relationship. As they bid farewell, the old man wished the young man a long and successful life.

Upon returning home to the wealthy man, suddenly, the affection decreased from the wealthy man. The young man began to question many things and started to suspect that the impoverished man might be his real father. While on the way back to school, his mother called him at night, crying. She confessed her mistakes of not being transparent about informing him of his real biological father. The man he met is indeed his biological father, and not the wealthy man who raised and provided for him to the point where he had reached.

This mistake of the mother psychologically affected the young man because, after learning the truth, he struggled to decide whom to love and whom to resent. He asked himself these questions: Why did my mother hide this from me? Why did my biological father abandon me? Why did this wealthy man claim to be my father when he was not? He questioned whom he should love and whom to resent. What is the fate of my life?

How would you handle this lack of transparency and the mistake caused by your parent/parents if you were in this situation?

One mistake, whether intentional or unintentional, can cost the well-being of your entire life and that of your entire generation. Lack of transparency and truth has led to significant discord and disintegration in many families today. Therefore, it is essential for families to consider transparency as a fundamental value, as the absence of transparency in a family has many detrimental effects.

In today's world, some men and women keep their assets undisclosed to their spouses and families in general. For example, money in banks, land, houses, farms, shops, etc. The Controller and Auditor General's Report for the Government of Tanzania for the fiscal year 2019/2020 states that money in bank accounts that remains unused for 15 years, along with money in financial accounts of mobile phones unused for five consecutive years, is considered unwanted funds and abandoned property according to the laws of the Bank of Tanzania. Therefore, all commercial banks and mobile network companies are required to return these funds to the Bank of Tanzania regularly. Additionally, in that report, the Controller and Auditor General identified a total of 12.5 billion Tanzanian shillings held by the central bank as abandoned funds.[13]

A pertinent question to ask is: If this man or woman who concealed these valuable assets were to pass away, who would benefit? Would it be the family, or would the assets be lost? If the family were to discover that their father had significant wealth that could have provided them with a comfortable life even after his death, what do you think their lasting sentiments would be? Let us strive to be honest and transparent in relationships, marriages, families, work, business, travel, education, and religion. However, it is crucial that parents and caregivers consistently encourage a culture of transparency in children, setting an example themselves. If children are not taught the value of transparency, they may hide many things that could, at times, lead to harm in their lives.

13. Masare, *How Unclaimed Billions Goes*, paras. 2–14.

ACCOUNTABILITY

The term "accountability" means something or an action that a person is obligated to do.[14] This interpretation aligns with the perspective that, accountability implies that individuals assigned responsibilities must fulfill those duties in ways consistent with accepted standards of behavior and conduct, and they will face consequences for failing to do so.[15] Therefore, based on Grant and Keohane's interpretation, it is evident that a significant characteristic defining any living being, especially humans, is the presence of responsibilities.

The concept of accountability for any human being begins as soon as they become mentally aware. Accountability is a crucial pillar in enhancing the well-being of the family. Every family has a substantial responsibility to instill a sense of accountability in all family members, particularly in raising and nurturing children in the principles of responsibility. This is a vital value in families, communities, and the nation as a whole.

In her explanation, Spellings states: "As parents, we all want our children to grow up to be responsible citizens and good people. We want them to learn to feel, think and act with respect for themselves and for other people. We want them to pursue their own well-being, while also being considerate of the needs and feelings of others. We want them to recognize and honor the democratic principles upon which our country was founded. We want them, in short, to develop strong character."[16] According to Spellings's perspective, it illustrates how every parent in the family has a responsibility to ensure that their child/children grow up as responsible citizens. Parents have a responsibility in the family to ensure their children grow with the ability to think and act respectfully in all their affairs for their own benefit and for the benefit of others. Children raised with a foundation of accountability have the opportunity to recognize and respect the principles of their

14. BAKITA, *Kamusi Kuu ya Kiswahili*, 1179.

15. Grant & Keohane, *Accountability and Power Abuses*. 29–30.

16. Spellings, *Foreword*, ii.

citizenship as established in their country. It is crucial for children to be taught about the concept of accountability as soon as they become mentally aware. They should also be taught to work, respect the laws of the country and their culture, participate in social activities, and appreciate the humanity and feelings of their fellow human beings.

This should go hand in hand with assigning age-appropriate tasks and responsibilities, considering their age and health conditions. This means they should not be given tasks that exceed their age and capabilities or overloaded with multiple tasks simultaneously. Therefore, it is evident that if a family fails to fulfill its responsibility, especially in instilling the values/principles of accountability and managing those principles, it is an undeniable truth that we will have a weak family and, ultimately, a nation of laziness in all aspects.

CONFLICT MANAGEMENT

In any environment, institution or organization, conflict cannot be avoided due to differences among individuals' ideas, desires, perceptions and needs.[17] According to Bilqis, conflict in the story can be divided into three types. First, conflict within a person (figure). This conflict is often called psychological conflict which is usually in the form of a person's struggle against himself, so that he can overcome and determine what he will do. Second, conflict between people or a person and society. This conflict is often called social conflict (social conflict), which is usually in the form of character conflicts, in relation to social problems. Third, conflicts between humans and nature. This conflict is often referred to as physical or element conflict (natural conflict), which usually arises when the character cannot control or utilize and civilize the surrounding environment as they should. Conflict is a state where people lack agreement, leading to disorder, violence, turmoil, disputes,

17. Hussein & Al-Mamary, *Conflicts, Types and Effects*, 1.

and ultimately the creation of differences.[18] If an individual can experience personal conflicts, having conflicts and differences within a family, which comprises multiple individuals, becomes an unavoidable occurrence. From this definition of conflicts, it is undeniable that conflict management is crucial in society as it touches individuals personally, families, and the community at large. This is equivalent to saying that no human being can isolate themselves from conflicts since it is an inherent disagreements in relationships exist between all human beings.[19]

Conflict management involves avoiding conflicts, dealing with conflict situations, and fostering cooperation and understanding between conflicting parties.[20] Family disagreements have two sides: negativity and positivity. This implies that there is conflict or a state of disagreement that can lead to either positive or negative outcomes in the family. Discussing the issue of disagreement or conflicts in the family, Thakore discloses that every relationship involves conflicts because it is an inherent among human beings.[21] The results in the study done by Aye, Akaneme, Adimora, Offorka, Robinson, Nwosu and Ekwealor, indicated that infertility, financial difficulties, poor communication between family members, lack of sexual satisfaction/gratification can lead to conflict in the family. Family conflicts inflict people for the course of their life and prevent them from experiencing their full potential.[22] In this situation, they concluded that people need to adopt conflict management strategies to reduce rifts and frictions that may lead to violence.[23]

Conflicts in a family have significant, often negative, effects. Examples of these effects include family division into factions, family members developing animosity, or even engaging in witchcraft

18. Bilqis, *Literature Review*, 4.

19. Thakore, *Conflict and Conflict Management*, 7.

20. Madalina, *Conflict Management*, 810.

21. Thakore, *Conflict and Conflict Management*, 7.

22. Aye, Akaneme, Adimora, Offorka, Robinson, Nwosu and Ekwealor, *Family Conflict and Managing Strategies*, 148.

23. *Ibid.* 158.

practices. Furthermore, when parents find themselves in conflicts, especially when their quarrels happen in front of their children, it causes substantial harm to the children mentally, physically, emotionally, psychologically, and in various other aspects.

The consequences of such quarrels include creating animosity among children towards their parents, instilling a spirit of revenge and retribution in children, making children grow up believing that violence in the family is an acceptable culture, creating disrespect among children towards their parents, prompting children to run away from home and move in with relatives or even living on the streets, making children lose interest in having their families (entering into marriages) when they become adults, and depriving children of the future due to a lack of essential social needs such as food, clothing, health, education, etc.

Now, let's listen to this true story that happened to one of my students in a certain region in Tanzania:

I had a student who was performing well in his studies at school. However, at some point, he began to experience a significant decline in his academic performance, much to the surprise of the school community that was aware of his excellent academic abilities. Following this decline, teachers started blaming him, alleging that he had joined bad groups, and that was the reason for his academic downfall. The teachers subjected him to severe corporal punishment, especially among students who performed poorly in exercises and exams. The teachers believed that physical punishment and scolding would make him regret his bad behavior and bring about a change, but the situation only worsened.

One day, I called the student, and we sat in a quiet place, just the two of us. I pleaded with him to tell me why his academic performance had declined to such an unexpected level, and why the teachers seemed to dislike him, associating him with bad groups. The student burst into tears, and I comforted him, telling him not to cry and to feel free to share anything that was troubling him. With sadness, he gave the following explanation:

"Teacher, whenever I am at home for a long time, I cannot study. The home environment is not peaceful. My parents, for a very long time, have been constantly quarreling. This father is not my biological father; my mother got married to him when I was already born from another father who abandoned me, and I lived with my mother in her family, in poverty. When my mother married this man, she called me, and I started living with her immediately after she had children with him. My mother is educating me while living with this man, although he does not like it. So, in their conflicts, I am not happy seeing my biological mother being beaten by this man. I find myself heavily involved in their disputes while defending my biological mother, who I believe is a significant support in achieving my dreams. In this environment, I find it difficult to study at home, and even when I come to school, I constantly worry about what will happen tonight at home. Therefore, I have many thoughts, to the point that even in class, I do not understand what is being taught. This is the reason for my decline academically, not involvement in bad groups. Teacher, what advice do you have for me? My heart hurts as I decline academically and witness my parents quarreling. I don't know what my future will be like." The student spoke with tears of pain.

After listening to him, I advised him to ask his parents to allow him to stay at a friend's place to study. I told him to focus on his life and not get involved in resolving the stepfather's conflicts with her biological mother since they are adults who met when he was not present, and he does not know the details of their disputes.

The student listened to my advice and implemented it. Eventually, he found himself improving academically, and I supported him throughout. He successfully completed his studies

and proceeded to university, where he pursued law. Currently,
he is a lawyer.

Due to this true story, it is clear that parental conflicts have significant consequences for children in their development. From this narrative, I learn that teachers and caregivers, in general, should not attack or punish children when they make mistakes before sitting down with them in a friendly manner and asking the cause of their mistakes. Even when we discipline them, it should be done with love, explaining the reasons for the discipline and its purpose.

Problem-solving and control should be considered essential foundations to build the well-being of a family from one generation to another. Just as we lock the doors of our houses and continue with activities inside without outsiders seeing what is happening, similarly, the issue of family conflicts should be handled within the family and not publicly disclosed to avoid giving unnecessary advantages to unrelated individuals. However, if the conflict becomes severe to the extent that the family cannot resolve it, it is crucial for the family to, through a specific procedure, involve psychologists, conflict resolution experts, or wise individuals in the community who can maintain the confidentiality of the conflicting parties to ensure that the conflict is controlled and harmony prevails.

To maintain this value in the family for family well-being, it is essential for the family to establish a system of meetings to discuss various family matters. These family meetings play a significant role in reducing the accumulation of various sources of conflicts within the family. Therefore, it is evident that a family without a culture of controlling conflicts and passing on this culture to its generations cannot be excellent and stable.

Furthermore, parents in a family should pass on this culture to their children to avoid negative conflicts and, instead, build their capacity to deal with positive conflicts.

INTEGRITY

BAKIZA and BAKITA interpret the term "integrity" as the state of doing justice without leaning to one side, or the behavior of acting justly without favoring any side, meaning fairness, justice, or honesty.[24] [25] Additionally, in line with this interpretation, Huberts comments that "integrity" has become a concept with more prominence in research on government and governance, as well as in actual policy making at all levels.[26] Hence, he has defined it as the quality of acting in accordance or harmony with relevant moral values, norms, and rules, a choice based partly on some of the arguments already put forward.[27] These interpretations provide a summary of integrity, implying caring for people, respecting time, working following established laws, rules, and regulations, avoiding acts of corruption and misappropriation of public assets, being truthful, working diligently, and knowledgeably.

Based on this interpretation, it is clear that integrity is a crucial value in life, not just for families but for everyone in society and the nation at large. Due to the sensitivity of this value, each family should set the foundations of integrity for all family members from one generation to another to have a better and stronger family and ultimately, a better society and nation. Additionally, parents and caregivers at the family level should teach the value of integrity to their children. You cannot talk about and encourage integrity in an adult who was not taught integrity by their parents from a young age. This truth is confirmed by the familiar Swahili saying that goes, "samaki mkunje angali mbichi" (fold a fish while it's still fresh).

Now, let's listen to the true story of my student in a certain region here in Tanzania.

---

24. BAKIZA, *Kamusi ya Kiswahili Fasaha*, 409.

25. BAKITA, *Kamusi Kuu ya Kiswahili*, 1064.

26. Huberts, What is Integrity? 1.

27. *Ibid.* 3.

In 2008, the term 'Corruption' gained significant attention among Tanzanians after a report on the embezzlement of public funds was presented in parliament by a special committee investigating the Richmond scandal, led by Member of Parliament for Kyela, Dr. Harrison Mwakyembe. According to the report, what implicated the then-Prime Minister of the United Republic of Tanzania, the Late Honorable Edward Lowasa in the Richmond scandal wasn't ownership, but rather, it appeared that as the Prime Minister, he was involved in overseeing the process of awarding the tender to the company. Following this report, Honorable Mr. Lowasa, resigned due to the allegations raised by the committee.

One day, I advised my students, asking them if they were aware of what was happening in our nation regarding the protection of public assets and finances. I asked, "When you become prominent leaders, will you do the same?" I posed this question without considering whether the allegations were true or false. One student responded, saying:

"Teacher, I will study finance and economics extensively so that I can excel. Once I've excelled, I will make sure to become a big corrupt person, embezzling a lot of government money and assets because by the time we finish our studies and get jobs, others will have already taken a significant portion of the funds. Government money belongs to everyone, and no one person owns it, so you can't leave it untouched if you find a way to take it. Just go for it, everyone is looking out for themselves and their families."

After hearing this student's words, I truly believed that there are individuals in society with a perspective similar to this student, which poses a serious danger to the well-being of the community and the nation as a whole. However, I took the time to teach him the importance of integrity and its benefits for

*himself, his family, his community, and his nation as a whole,
and he understood it well.*

In the account of this student, I learned that he doesn't encounter messages that encourage him to be honest in everything
he does. A student like him poses a challenge to teach integrity,
especially when he is already an adult and is being taught by someone who is not his parent.

This emphasizes the crucial need for parents/guardians and
teachers to strive to demonstrate integrity in everything they do.
Subsequently, they should impart this value to their children so
that it becomes their habit even as they engage in their daily responsibilities as they grow.

PATRIOTISM

Patriotism is a crucial value in the family, society, and nation.
When we discuss patriotism, we move beyond biological relationships within the family to the national level, where we consider social, political, economic, and diplomatic relationships among the
citizens of a country, rooted in their families. BAKITA describes
patriotism as an individual's deep love for their country (citizenship, nationality) to the extent that they are willing to die to defend
it.[28] Similarly, Nincic and Ramos define patriotism as Patriotism
involves attachment to a country, an entity that includes both the
social group and the existing norms and institutions which are the
foundation for the existing state.[29] Therefore, it can be said that
true patriotism should begin in the family, as it is within the family
that the first citizen is nurtured. Anyone aspiring to advocate for
the interests of the many, especially those not bound by blood ties,
must first demonstrate their proficiency in defending their own
family.

---

28. BAKITA, *Kamusi Kuu ya Kiswahili*, 1182.

29. Nincic & Ramos, *The Dynamics of Patriotism*, 6.

In the Bible, there are words that state, "But if anyone does not provide for his relatives, and especially for members of his household, he has denied the faith and is worse than an unbeliever (1 Tim 5:8)." This biblical quote aligns with a quote from the Holy Quran, in the first chapter called 'SURAH AL-FAATIHA,' verse 5, which emphasizes the importance of people not living in isolation but being together in all good things. It also highlights the necessity of making efforts to reconcile with others to ensure collective safety.

These quotes demonstrate that a person cannot be patriotic to their community and nation without first displaying patriotism within their family. However, it is crucial to transfer the patriotism rooted in the family and affirm it at the societal and national levels for the greater good, eliminating selfishness within the community and the nation as a whole.

In today's world, many people seem to prioritize selfish interests, especially when considering the interests of the many as we transition from the family to the community and the nation at large. This has eroded the concept of patriotism for the country, and consequently, even patriotism within the family is affected, as the well-being of the family depends on the well-being of the nation as a responsible entity for the protection and prosperity of the family. Therefore, true patriotism is that which begins in the family and persists in the community and nation as a whole from one generation to another as a crucial value. The significant emphasis here is on how parents should teach their children about patriotism and its significance at the family, community, and national levels. I still believe that the family remains the only institution capable of providing training that can build a child's well-being and that of their generation if such training is effectively imparted.

SELF-CONFIDENCE

Self-confidence is the state of having a heart without doubt in one's abilities or knowledge.[30] In the same contour, Perkins describe self-confidence, as an overarching latent Construct which is mainly influenced by three factors: self-efficacy, self-esteem, and self-compassion. Together, these constructs determine how trustworthy an individual considers themselves to be, and how much they trust themselves (i.e., Internal Self-confidence). While one's attitude towards themselves is undoubtedly important, subtle signals and behaviors (i.e., External Self-Confidence) are thought to be indicative of an individual's level of self-confidence—and therefore inform others' perceptions of their competence.[31] Unlike self-confidence, fear, doubt, and anxiety are significant enemies of self-confidence and prevalent challenges faced by many individuals, both young and old, in their daily lives. A lack of self-confidence in life has severe consequences for human beings, especially when a person hesitates to undertake activities that could contribute to their progress. Hence, in my view, in our current lives, we need self-confidence and significant self-esteem more than ever in human history. However, despite advancements and the vast knowledge and understanding of various matters by humans, there is still fear that prevents individuals from being confident and leading their lives as they deserve.

I suggest that there are many factors that can undermine a person's self-confidence, making them feel inferior in various aspects of life. Sometimes, this lack of confidence prevents individuals from accomplishing tasks they are knowledgeable about and perform daily. Psychologically, this is a condition that can affect a person's capabilities; although physically able, they may struggle to utilize their abilities due to a lack of self-confidence. Therefore, building self-confidence is not a short-term endeavor; it requires long-term practice. In my view, some practices may include the following:

30. BAKITA, *Kamusi Kuu ya Kiswahili*, 1107.

31. Perkins, *Integrated Model of Self-Confidence*, 188.

a. Getting accustomed to sitting in the front row during gatherings and making eye contact without fear when communicating with others.

b. Walking briskly with confidence, avoiding sluggishness or hesitancy.

c. Practicing speaking in front of people, especially when presenting arguments on a specific subject.

d. Accepting oneself first.

e. Properly preparing for tasks and events and avoiding blame games.

These techniques can serve as a foundation for building self-confidence in the daily lives of individuals. Self-confidence is a crucial value in an individual's personal life, family, society, and the nation as a whole. As previously mentioned, due to a lack of self-confidence, many people have been deprived of their fundamental rights in their daily lives. Any human lacking confidence in their actions cannot succeed in their life, and they will consistently depend on others for many tasks.

The primary agent for building self-confidence in an individual is their family, through parents and caregivers. Alongside the family, other agents that can contribute to building an individual's self-confidence include educational institutions, religious organizations, political parties, cooperative societies, civil society organizations, age groups, sports, and entertainment. Through these agents, I believe the foundation of self-confidence in an individual's life within the family, society, and the nation as a whole can be strengthened. Therefore, it is evident that this is a crucial value in the family. The absence of this value leads to families characterized by fear, doubt, and anxiety in their daily activities, creating a dependent family, which poses significant risks to the well-being of the family, the society they live in, and the nation as a whole.

The key emphasis here is on parents, caregivers, and school teachers ensuring that they nurture self-confidence in children at all times, in any place, under any circumstance, without crossing

legally known boundaries and without disrespecting or dishon-
oring anyone based on race, age, ethnicity, nationality, religion,
education level, standard of living, or gender.

FAITH IN RELIGION

The distinguishing line between spirituality, religion, and faith can
become fuzzy. To some, it would seem that they would be inter-
changeable. Some authors in this issue use them synonymously.[32]
However, in his model, Newman insisted that, spirituality and religion are a function of faith. Both religion and spirituality require
faith as a foundation. In other words, faith is the guiding principle
by which individuals are either religious or spiritual. Faith serves
as both the source and the target of their religion or spirituality.[33]

Whenever we talk about believing in religion, we mean
trusting, fearing, and respecting God in everything we do every
day, as religion is the plan to seek and worship the Almighty God
known among many people. Not everyone in the world believes
in the existence of God, and it is not necessary to believe in the
existence of God. However, a significant percentage of people
worldwide believe in God. This truth does not require validation
through research because, in the ordinary experience of life, many
people are heard using various words as a significant indication of
the manifestation of God's presence. These words include phrases
such as "let's pray to God for help," "let's trust God; He will help
us," "I'm sorry, and may God heal you," "God is there," "God is not
indifferent," and "God does not forsake His servant." These phrases
and others are often uttered by believers and even non-believers.

Rotilă[set hacek over a] describe that, human existence is
based on a system of beliefs in a world structure, which is essential
for survival. Religion is one of the integrators of these systems.[34]
Various religious explanations indicate that, once purified from

32. Newman, *Faith, Spirituality, and Religion*, 105.

33. *Ibid.* 106.

34. Rotilă[set hacek over a], *Religion and Society*, 126.

ignorance and sin resulting from superstition, humans, in their natural state, were convinced that there is a God, the creator of all, on whom the world and our experiences depend. In addition to these explanations, Rotilă[set hacek over a] states that religion is an atypical social contract: you did not initiate and sign it, but you are born into it, adhering to its provisions through behaviour; alternatives are often few.[35] Since the spiritual manifestation of humans regarding the existence of God has endured historically, we can say that the concept of Divinity is part of human culture and that this concept carries a significant orientation for entire societies and their people.

Therefore, religious freedom in human life has been seen as the number one human right, and the quest for God for worship has been considered the number one duty of humans, regardless of the type and system of the respective religion. Based on these explanations, it is evident that building faith in religion is a historical matter and is part of human life, aiming to construct a morally upright society since God is the father of ethics.

In fact, God is the founder of all living and visible things and that He is the fulfillment of our expectations for happiness as human beings. For example, in the Bible, there are words that say, *"The fear of the Almighty is the beginning of knowledge. The fear of the Almighty is to hate evil. I hate pride, arrogance, evil behavior, and perverse speech" (Prov 1:7; 8:13)*. In line with these words, as explained in the Holy Bible, similarly, in the stories of the Prophet Muhammad in the Holy Qur'an, as narrated by Maina, it is stated: *"Acquire knowledge; he who acquires knowledge in the way of the Almighty performs an act of godliness. He who speaks the praises of the Lord performs an act of worship. He who seeks these does an act of valuable sacrifice. He who teaches people to respect and fear God performs an act of worship to God."*[36]

All the words mentioned in the Holy Bible and the Holy Qur'an clearly show that God abhors any form of evil and is pleased

---

35. Ibid.

36. Maina, *Muslim Education in Kenya*, 44.

with all people who respect God. Believing in Him is a significant asset for a life of righteousness.

Thus, a family that can build its foundation on religious faith aimed at helping individuals do everything while fearing to act against God's will, whose primary foundation is righteousness, will be a better and stronger family. Religious faith in an individual's life, if considered by parents and caregivers and passed on to children in their upbringing, is believed to be a crucial value in building a family, and ultimately, a society and a nation with morals and righteousness.

CONCLUSION

Due to the in-depth discussion about philosophy and family values, as the author has illustrated in this chapter, there is no doubt that this is the guide to the heritage of every family, especially in these times of globalization. If every family invests in this heritage, it is certain that our society will have a better generation despite the challenges of globalization. It is true that many families strive to leave a legacy of education and wealth for their generation, but without passing on these values to our children, this education and wealth will not benefit them.

The truth remains that many parents who bequeathed their children a legacy of education and wealth without passing on these values have not been helpful. These values, in general, are the wisdom that can guide any human of any status, type, age, or gender to live a better life in their family, community, and nation.

I therefore conclude by saying that we should leave these words (philosophy/values) to our children; they are the key to an unquestionably good life in the society they have and will live in on this planet, especially in these times of globalization.

DISCUSSION QUESTIONS:

(i) Explain your understanding of the difference between philosophy and values.

(ii) In your perspective, do you think there is one value that is better than others? Provide reasons to defend your viewpoint.

CHAPTER 3

General Responsibilities of a Family

INTRODUCTION

THE GENERAL RESPONSIBILITIES OF a family are the lifeblood of any family. This is equivalent to saying that a family is a relationship with agreements, and its foundation lies in how it fulfills its duties in taking care of its members. Unfortunately, in these times of globalization, many people have established family relationships without a foundation for fulfilling responsibilities. This issue particularly affects many young people who enter family relationships without preparing to fulfill family duties.

As a result, among Tanzanian society and other African and global communities at large, we have witnessed an increase of many parents failing to fulfill their family responsibilities, especially in the upbringing of children. Many children have been abandoned in the hands of elderly grandparents who are unable to provide proper care and upbringing. This has contributed to the rise of many children living on the streets and engaging in hazardous activities, especially in urban areas, not only in Tanzania but also in many developing countries around the world.

Thus, the significant duty of every family is to ensure the presence and sufficiency of the general family needs. These needs include food, shelter and clothing, ensuring good family relationships, proper upbringing, safety, and social services such as quality education and healthcare for the well-being of the family itself. These responsibilities are specified and discussed in detail as follows:

RESPONSIBILITY FOR FOOD

For any human to live well, he/she must eat food/nutrition, and not just any food but nutritious food. This means that not every food a human eats qualifies to be called of good nutrition. Nutrition has been defined in the health policy document of 2007 of Tanzania as the totality of various steps, starting from when the food is eaten to how our bodies absorb and use nutrients to provide the consumer with good health. While good nutrition comes from proper eating, meaning sufficient and well-balanced food; poor nutrition leads to malnutrition, which causes health problems that can result in a person losing their mental capacity.[1] Therefore, according to this policy, we cannot separate good health from good nutrition.

Every human eats food, especially nutritious food, to live and not just to consume food but to fulfill their dreams as they were created. In human life, food is crucial as it helps build good health, a vital pillar enabling any human to think well in fulfilling their responsibilities. The absence of food in a family leads to various problems such as misunderstandings among family members, betrayal within the family, contempt between family members, children running away from the family and becoming street beggars, and sometimes the complete breakdown of family relationships.

Considering the importance of food in human life, it is the responsibility of every family to ensure the sufficiency of good food for the well-being of the family. It should be understood that food is the primary need of every family worldwide. However, the emphasis in this responsibility is for every family leader to ensure that special groups such as children, elderly grandparents, and

---

1. Jamhuri ya Muungano wa Tanzania, *Sera ya Afya*, 14.

helpless disabled individuals receive adequate and quality food without any worries or discrimination.

RESPONSIBILITY FOR SHELTER

Shelter is the second basic need in human life globally. After working, a person needs a place to rest to have time to reflect on various matters, and they also need a peaceful and secure place. According Hurtubise, Babin and Grimard, the definition of a shelter is no less problematic. In its initial sense, a shelter is a place where one goes to avoid danger, an inconvenience or a place where people who have no place else to go or want to go can gather.[2] Shelter is mentioned as a crucial need to human being because it is a protection and provides us with a sense of safety and a place where our families connect. What I can say is that, shelter is also associated with other issues we consider as part of normal life, such as privacy, freedom, respect, and safety. Hence, shelter is a fundamental basis for the comfort and happiness of many human rights.

Now it should be born in everyone's mind that, when any human lacks shelter, it means they lack protection, safety, relationships, privacy, freedom, respect, comfort, and happiness in any human right. In simple terms, when a person lacks shelter, it means they have lost the value of living on this earth as a living being, and instead, they are equated to any other living creature, such as a dog, cat, rat, lion, fish, etc., and this is not the purpose of human creation.

A family without proper shelter is at risk, and especially the large group of victims includes children, elderly grandparents, and helpless disabled individuals because the safety of their protection largely depends on proper accommodation.

However, it is an undeniable truth that poor shelter significantly contributes to the suppression of one's thoughts, especially for children in the process of growth. When a person feels inferior due to their living conditions, they lack confidence in what they

2. Hurtubise, Babin & Grimard, *Understanding Shelters*, 1.

think and believe, and even when they encounter opportunities, they lack the faith to seize them, believing they will face obstacles based on their perceived inadequacy. It is the responsibility of every family to ensure they have proper shelter for their well-being because good shelter is the health and protection of any human being.

RESPONSIBILITY FOR CLOTHING

The oldest remains of clothing recovered by archaeologists are a few cloth fragments that date from 12,000 years ago at the end of the last ice age. However, clothing was invented much earlier, beginning perhaps a million years ago, and its prehistoric development was limited to populations in cool environments.[3] Textiles began to replace animal skins as the preferred material for clothes from the end of the last ice age 12,000 years ago, based on thermal properties of woven fabric which permit perspiration to escape more easily. Fabric was a practical and comfortable material for people who continued to use clothes in the warmer and more humid weather conditions.[4] Now, Li, Liu, Li, Li, Xu, and Tao disclose the three dimensions to understand the essence of clothing. One is to regard clothing as the need of human survival and development, which came into being when human society developed to a certain social stage. Thus, it can be revealed that the origin of clothing is the result of existence determining consciousness. Second, clothing is seen as the requirement of human aesthetic art, which appeared as an aesthetic object when it entered the society, whereby under this dimension, the origin of clothing was the result of aesthetic consciousness. Third, clothing is regarded as the psychological needs of human beings, whose origin is to meet the psychological needs of individual differences of human beings, which ultimately leads to the conclusion that consciousness determines the existence.[5]

3. Gilligan, *Encyclopedia of Evolutionary Psychological Science*, 2.
4. Ibid, 3.
5. Li, Liu, Li, Li, Xu & Tao, *Origin of Clothing*, 654.

Li and others informed that, there are more than ten academic viewpoints on the origin of clothing. The representative ones are Body Protection Theory, Theory of Warm-keeping, Sexual Attraction Theory, Shame Theory, Decorative Theory, etc.[6]

Based on Li and his fellow scholars, I understand that, the theory of clothing reflects a diverse perspective including that one of preserving an individual's dignity and honor according to the cultural norms of their society. Additionally, I have learnt that, clothing is a source of protection against the effects of weather. Oladipo discloses that, clothes speak louder than words. One of the distinctive features of human clothing is that a group of people share particular pattern of dress and the development of these complex and varied cultural patterns characterize human society. Clothing could be referred to as non – verbal communication, but yet it communicates. Clothing carries messages and conveys vital information about people; when you meet an individual or group of people for the first time, you can easily form an impression of that person from the information convey to you by his/her appearance (cloth). That is; the social background, the kind of job they do, and even what kind of person they are.[7] Hence, based on Oladipo's description, it is true that, the type of clothing a person wears also plays a significant role in identifying their character and mental state. Oladipo has summarized the functions of clothes in terms of social functions, status or identification with one's social group, psychological functions, cultural functions, religious functions, physical functions, ethnic and political functions, beauty/ seductive functions and moral functions of clothing.[8] Based on the explanations and emphasis built by scholars in discussing the importance of clothing for humans, it is clear that any human, whether sane or not, loses their human value when lacking appropriate clothing.

In fulfilling this responsibility, many families tend to forget or intentionally deny their children the right to wear clothing that

6. *Ibid.* 651.

7. Oladipo, *Functions of Traditional Dress*, 69.

8. *Ibid*, 71–77.

fully covers their bodies. It is common to encounter many children, especially in rural areas, walking half-naked or completely naked. Some parents leave their children like this due to the inability to afford clothing for them. Moreover, others have the financial means to buy clothes for their children but do not prioritize purchasing appropriate clothing, as they see no problem with their children going naked. They might even claim that children do not have any issues being naked because they are not aware of the shame associated with nudity. The truth is that this is a violation of human dignity. Here, I would like to urge parents to ensure they buy decent clothes for their children, covering their bodies and giving them the respect they deserve, just like adults.

Furthermore, it is the responsibility of every family to ensure that all its members, regardless of age, gender, mental state, have suitable clothing at all times, considering the cultural norms and traditions of their community.

RESPONSIBILITY FOR RELATIONSHIPS AND COMMUNICATION

Any sane person needs to relate to and communicate with their fellow human beings in their surrounding environment. Good communication and relationships at the family level are the foundation of the well-being of any family worldwide. Relationship experts in family matters, Fahey, Keilthy, and Polek, explain that the structure and effective communication between family members are the basis of a lively family and the catalyst for the well-being of parents and children in the family.[9]

In a family, every family member has the responsibility to relate to and communicate with each other, regardless of age, gender, beliefs, education, tribe, or race. Good relationships and communication anywhere are the bridge and foundation of development and prosperity in any society worldwide. Good relationships and communication in a family greatly help in sharing burdens among

9. Fahey, Keilthy & Polek, *Family Relationships and Well-Being*, 12.

family members. If this responsibility is fulfilled properly, the family will be in a state of love, unity, solidarity, and free from conflicts. Thus, every family should fulfill this responsibility completely.

RESPONSIBILITY FOR PROPER UPBRINGING OF CHILDREN

No adult person has grown up without being a child first. Everyone is a child to their parent(s), even if they have gray hair, they still remain a child to those parents. Therefore, a child should be respected and raised well because they are the foundation of an adult, and without a child, there is no adult.

There are many proverbs that express the concept of upbringing; for example, "Train up a child in the way he should go: and when he is old, he will not depart from it" (Holy Bible, Proverbs 22:6). Similarly, the Qur'an in Surah Al-Baqara, verse 216 emphasizes the need to pay close attention to a child's customs and behaviors, avoiding them from committing wrongs according to their desires or being treated too harshly, which might lead them to lose heart. A person's behavior, whether good or bad, is significantly related to the type of upbringing they received as a child.

The future life system of any child is a result of the training and upbringing they received in their childhood. Any perspective that parents develop regarding certain behaviors for a child and solidify is challenging to erase when they become adults. The philosopher in literature, Achebe, corroborate as he says that people look at their leaders as role models to be followed, and their followers imitate their actions, behaviors, and attitudes. The philosopher emphasizes that a leader without good discipline will be reflected in their followers. [10]

In analyzing Achebe's philosophy, Uwe, Asuquo, and Ekuri dissect the concept of leadership at the family level by portraying parents as leaders within the family. They explain that if parents are seen as role models by their children, they should not have

---

10. Achebe, *The Trouble with Nigeria*. 31.

bad behavior because their behavior will be the behavior of their children, who are their followers imitating their behavior as their leaders.[11] The issue of parenting and the type of upbringing that parents should provide to their children, especially considering their future, is a responsibility that requires very high attention.

A child is built as a good member of society within the family. It is only in the family that a child starts to be shaped as a complete person morally. If the family fails in its duty to prepare the child as a good member of society from childhood, then the resulting society from that child will likely have a high failure rate.

In his analysis of policy and research, a researcher from HakiElimu, Zombwe, says: *"It is an obvious fact that the success of an adult is influenced by the upbringing in childhood along with the interaction of the environment and society. If parents or guardians make an effort to build a child and prepare them to be a conscientious citizen who is self-aware, it is quite evident that the contribution of such an individual to the development of their community will be significant, and their family will benefit more. The growth and development of a child are influenced by how parents and the family and society mold the child towards achieving the desired well-rounded development."*[12] Therefore, based on Zombwe's explanation, I can say that the family has a great responsibility and duty to ensure it provides good upbringing for the child, considering the good customs and traditions of the community around them. The crucial thing is that the child should be built mentally, physically, and spiritually to grow as a mentally capable, confident, and righteous person throughout their life.

RESPONSIBILITY FOR DEFENSE AND SECURITY

The issue of defense and security is crucial and should be considered by everyone, especially families, as it is a fundamental right for every individual. A person or family without defense

---

11. Uwe, Asuquo & Ekuri, *Parenting and Responsibility*, 51–57
12. Zombwe, *Kudumisha Haki za Watoto*, 1.

and security strategies is at risk of extinction, as without protection and security, there is no life for any being. Every human being should first protect themselves and ensure their safety at any cost before being protected by anyone or anything. This does not apply to young children, as they cannot defend themselves and need to be protected at any cost from potential dangers.

According to the report released by the Commission for Human Security, the security of any human being is emphasized to be of utmost importance. The security of any human is considered a crucial pillar in protecting all essential aspects of human life, contributing to their freedom and the fulfillment of their life. According to the commission, every human being has the responsibility to protect themselves and be protected against any potential danger for the safety of their lives.[13]

The commission goes further to indicate that an enhanced human security allows individuals to enjoy politics, society, environment, economy, military, and cultural systems that collectively provide them with the opportunity to live, sustain themselves, and be respected.[14] Therefore, based on the explanations provided by the commission on the issue of defense and security, every family has a significant responsibility to ensure the defense and security of its members.

In this era of rapid technological advancements and globalization, security risks for humans, especially children, are increasing. Technology is being misused to exploit young children, leading to cyberbullying and abuse. Additionally, malicious intent and actions against the safety of children are rapidly increasing. Acts of child rape are on the rise, posing a threat to the safety of children.

On October 6, 2017, the International Conference on the protection of young children in the "digital world," held in Vatican City, Rome, Italy, addressed these concerns under the theme "The Dignity of Young Children in the Digital World." The conference resulted in the adoption of the "Rome Declaration" as reported

13. Commission for Human Security, *Human Security in Theory*, 6.
14. *Ibid*, 7.

by Mjingwa. According to Mjingwa, the Rome Declaration states: "*The life of every child is unique, important, and of great value, and every child should be respected and valued in their humanity, receiving protection and security. However, today there are millions of children who lack protection and security. The significant progress of technology and its use in daily life continues to bring about substantial changes not only in people's actions but also in their identity. This is a great blessing. However, on the other hand, these developments have created a darkness entwined in the sea of social media, which leaves significant harm to the well-being and growth of young children.*"[15] Therefore, considering the evident truth about limited security for young children in various areas, every individual, not only within families but also in society at large, has the responsibility to protect children at any cost from all types of potential dangers. I urge parents to be vigilant and cautious about visitors to their homes, as there are both good and bad people. It is advisable not to let children share a room with guests. By doing this, the family and the community as a whole will have fulfilled the responsibility of defense and security completely.

RESPONSIBILITY FOR QUALITY EDUCATION

It is an undeniable fact that if there is a term "Excellent," then terms like "Non-excellent, subpar, or weak" are words that must exist behind the term excellent. Due to this reality, when discussing the concept of education, it is not accurate to talk about education in sufficiency without discussing what kind of education is excellent or non-excellent. Therefore, it is essential to ask ourselves the question: What does quality education mean? In answering this question, we may have various responses. For example, in its research titled "What is Quality Education?" the non-governmental organization focused on education issues in Tanzania, HakiElimu, was able to interpret the term quality education from four perspectives:

15. Mjingwa, *Tamko la Roma*, para. 2.

First: Quality education involves educational facilities such as the number of classrooms, libraries, laboratories, teacher houses, learning and teaching materials, and toilets.

Second: Quality education is related to the number of students who pass the examinations for completing primary education or those of Form 4 or 6. The participants' opinions in the research were that if students were passing exams well, the quality of education in that school was considered high, and if students were failing, then the quality was perceived as low.

Third: Quality education can be improved by enhancing the quality of teachers in schools. According to this perspective, a good teacher provides quality education.

Fourth: quality education is interpreted by looking at the level of a student's employability and their ability to participate in various social activities that impact the lives of those around them upon completing school.[16]

These four perspectives, as outlined by HakiElimu in their research, lay the foundation for the concept of quality education. These perspectives can form a collective view explaining the overall meaning of quality education, as described by the United Nations Children's Fund [UNICEF], that quality education includes:

i. Learners who are healthy, well-nourished and ready to participate and learn, and supported in learning by their families and communities;

ii. Environments that are healthy, safe, protective and gender-sensitive, and provide adequate resources and facilities;

iii. Content that is reflected in relevant curricula and materials for the acquisition of basic skills, especially in the areas of literacy, numeracy and skills for life, and knowledge in such areas as gender, health, nutrition, HIV/AIDS prevention and peace.

iv. Processes through which trained teachers use child-centred teaching approaches in well-managed classrooms and

16. HakiElimu, *Elimu Bora ni Nini?* 6–8.

schools and skillful assessment to facilitate learning and reduce disparities.

v. Outcomes that encompass knowledge, skills and attitudes,
and are linked to national goals for education and positive
participation in society.[17]

All the perspectives given about the concept of quality education
convince me to believe and state that quality education is not about
passing exams or having a good certificate, but it is about having
the ability to think, be confident, confront, and ultimately solve
the problems and challenges that you face for your own benefit
and the benefit of the society around you. Therefore, if this is the
concept of quality education, every child should be provided with
an environment by their parents or caregivers to obtain such education as part of their fundamental rights. In simple terms, I can
say that if children lack quality education, they have missed a pillar
of self-worth that makes them appear insignificant in their family
and community. Thus, it is the duty of the family to ensure that the
child receives quality education as their fundamental right.

RESPONSIBILITY FOR GOOD HEALTH

You cannot talk about the concept of good health without first
discussing the concept of health itself. This term can have various perspectives from professionals and various authorities. For
example, in the health policy of the United Republic of Tanzania,
the term "Health" is translated as the overall well-being of an individual physically, mentally, and socially, and the absence of diseases.[18] This interpretation stems from the definition provided by
the World Health Organization (WHO) in its 1948 constitution.[19]
Looking deeply into the translation of the term health, let us ask
ourselves, if the weight of the term health seems to be the same
as the life of a human being, what is the meaning of good health?

17. UNICEF, *Defining Quality in Education*, 4.

18. Jamhuri ya Muungano wa Tanzania, *Sera ya Afya*, 1.

19. World Health Organization, *World Health Organization Constitution*, 1.

A health expert from the European Commission on Health and Consumer Safety, Byrne, attempts to provide a definition of the term good health when he says that Good health is a state of physical and mental well-being necessary to live a meaningful, pleasant and productive life.[20] Based on Byrne's interpretation, what I can believe is that the correct interpretation of good health is to have good physical and mental well-being that allows an individual to live a meaningful life in society, a life full of happiness and contribution to resource production.

Therefore, parents, guardians, and families as a whole are responsible for ensuring that children in the family are raised with consideration for good health as one of the essential pillars in the child's upbringing. Without good health, it is challenging to describe a human being as thriving.

CONCLUSION

This chapter provides a realistic picture of the family in action, as its main purpose is to show an active family. This chapter is crucial in this book as it highlights the importance and responsibility of the family in raising a child who will be beneficial to the family, society, and the nation as a whole. It also provides significant lessons on what constitutes an ideal family that fulfills its responsibilities in the overall upbringing of a child, especially in these times of globalization where the family's upbringing system has changed. Additionally, it illustrates the necessary aspects for a family that seem to be the general responsibilities of an active family. However, the vitality of family life, like any other institution, is built on philosophy, values, and responsibilities that are the responsibility of each institution.

20. Byrne, *Good Health for All*, 1.

DISCUSSION QUESTIONS:

i. Discuss the differences between an active family and an inactive family.

ii. Discuss with examples the responsibilities of a family as outlined in this chapter.

CHAPTER 4

Management of Family Resources

INTRODUCTION

THE TERM RESOURCE CAN be interpreted in various perspectives depending on the context, expertise, philosophy, etc. According to Zlotin and Zusman, the term is broadly used in many contexts, signifying natural resources, financial resources, and human resources.[1] In their definition of the term "resource", Zlotin and Zusman first explain the history of the word's use, stating that the initial use of the term "resource" was related to natural resources such as water, land, trees, minerals, etc. For centuries, the abundance of natural resources was the primary criterion used to measure the power of a nation or region. Later, capitalism and the industrial revolution collectively led to the concept of human resources. In the second half of the twentieth century, the concept of human resources was established as a way of managing revolutions. Just as natural resources contribute significantly to nations in winning wars or facilitating economic excellence, financial resources and human resources were seen as means or factors in achieving market success. Many social theories have focused on and worked

1. Zlotin and Zusman, *The Concept of Resources*, 1.

within the context of natural resources, financial resources, and human resources.[2]

When discussing the term resource in general, many scholars and various professionals, theoretically based on the division of natural resources, financial resources, and human resources as described by Zlotin and Zusman, have explored and discussed these important resources that require effective management and maintenance. The author attempts to show and discuss some of these crucial resources available in various categories of the total resources, such as human resources, time resources, financial resources, and land resources. Each family has a significant responsibility in managing these resources thoroughly because a family that does not manage these resources jeopardizes its well-being.

HUMAN RESOURCES

Human resources can be interpreted in several ways; for example, Guest describe human resources as key assets that are there to be managed, utilized, or possibly exploited to improve organizational performance.[3] In my view, I see human resources as individuals within a company as the workforce, each utilizing their skills and abilities to contribute to the company's success Additionally, any one willing to sell their labor, knowledge, or time for compensation to enhance an institution is known as a human resource. Thus, when discussing family resources, all family members are considered the number one and most important resource, appreciated by anyone. A person is more valuable than anything in the family and should not be valued less than anything. Even holy books state that humans are more valuable than anything else because they are created in the image of the Almighty. For this reason, humans are given authority to rule over other resources such as animals, insects, land, trees, and water (Holy Bible, Gen 1:26–28).

2. *Ibid.* 2.

3. Guest, *HRM and Performance*, 52.

Due to the value that humans possess, managing and leading them requires very high attention, unlike leading a machine or something without will, as in the case of humans. Referring to Armstrong and Taylor, Bejtkovský explains that human resource management is a broad and essential technique that can be considered a philosophy on how to manage people.[4]

Therefore, I can say that a strong and stable family is one that cares for its members as valuable resources more than anything else. It prioritizes the interests of all family members and fights for all their rights at any cost without breaking the laws and regulations established in society and the nation where the family is located. Furthermore, it is essential for every family to take on the responsibility of building awareness within its generation about the importance and proper management of human resources for its prosperity.

TIME RESOURCES

The history of anything/living being, including humans, is rooted in time. Humans have a sense of time that enables them to count the lives of all things and the entire process of their growth, experiencing different eras. Time is an undervalued resource in many institutions, including the family. All activities, whether purchases, production, or the transfer of goods, involve time that often goes unmeasured except when it indicates the completion of a task or something similar. Moreover, time is a tangible measure showing how an institution can work efficiently and effectively. Productivity and its efficiency are influenced by time, such as buying and selling or the flow of money and labor.[5] In this regard, I can say that anything or any action that humans can undertake is bound by time and nothing else. Time is a crucial factor in all human activities and overall success. There is a saying that all successful people in life are slaves to the resource of time. Based

4. Bejtkovský, *Selected Current Trends*, 1833.
5. Kumar & Aithal, *Time as Strategic Resource*, 1138.

on my belief in the importance of time, I agree with this saying. Due to the significance of time, I can say that time is an essential resource, although many people are unaware that time is the great and essential engine for the fulfillment of all human activities. This resource is remarkable and unique because all humans, each in their way and environment, collectively use it to fulfill their various responsibilities. Humans abandon it as soon as they pass away. This resource cannot be grasped, preserved, or owned personally. It is the property of all people and is not restricted by the environment or climate.

Kenneth compares time to a very precious thing; it has wings and as such is passing very fast. Time Management "is a set of principles, practices, skills, tools and systems that help us use time to accomplish what we want. It refers to the techniques, and strategies that individuals use in utilizing and maximizing the work that they do. Managing time effectively helps to develop a better personality in an organization.[6] Additionally, he emphasizes that, time, once gone never comes back. In simple terms, I can say that time is an irreplaceable resource.[7]

Therefore, I emphasize that since we are bound by time, it is essential to consider time as a natural element directly linked to our minds, thoughts, and the fate of our lives in general. It is crucial for everything we do in families, communities, and nations as a whole, to be done with consideration for time. Without discipline over time, we cannot achieve our plans, and we may die, leaving responsibilities unfinished. Let us avoid meaningless sayings as we are used to hearing some people say, "I was wasting time," and instead invest in protecting time as an invaluable resource. The emphasis on this resource is that every institution, including the family, should invest in respecting time. Parents and guardians should build the capacity of children to respect and manage time through practical actions. Additionally, even in schools, teachers, who have ample time with children, should ensure that our children develop a habit of doing things with respect for time. This will

6. Keneth, *Importance of Time Management*, 2–3.

7. *Ibid*. 3.

help them achieve their dreams because any student who values time tends to have a disciplined attitude and can succeed in their studies.

FINANCIAL RESOURCES

Financial resources are the total financial sources available for use in an institution. According to Scholars from the University of York have described financial resources as funds and assets that finance an organisation's activities and investments. In simple terms, financial resources are the monies that keep a business operating, and there are several ways a business will raise and use its financial resources.[8] Additionally, they categorized financial resources into two categories. These are Internal sources of finance which include all funds that come from within a business. Examples include profits generated by the business, retained earnings, capital funding, and liquid assets. Liquid assets are business assets that can be easily converted into cash. The second category is external sources of finance which are funds that come from outside a business. Examples include loans and credit from external sources, such as banks.[9]

Financial resources are a valuable and precious resource. In human life on Earth, money appears to have great value, sometimes exceeding the value of the person who creates and uses it, even though fundamentally, this should not be assumed because humans have no alternative. This is due to some people appearing to prioritize financial interests over human dignity. Money has been given many names according to its importance in various daily uses of humans, for example, money is the soap of the soul, money is everything, money is life, money is the remedy for problems, etc. Social services such as health and education, basic human rights such as food, shelter, and clothing—all of these can be obtained or improved to fit in daily use depending on money.

8. University of York, *Financial Resources.*
9. Ibid.

Hence, money is the cornerstone of the economy because everything we do is sum up to money and every day we carry out a lot of financial operations, sometimes even without realizing .[10]

The importance of money is evident because thinking of money, I get to a point where I realize the importance of money in each field or domain of activity, a resource that is necessary, limited and not-renewable if not used accordingly. Additionally, the financial resources are very important for the entrepreneur alongside with ideas and a good management, thus creating a positive role and a fast expansion in companies' and countries' development, in which these tactics are applied on a short, medium and long term. Moreover, I insist that, money is a valuable resource. In other words, I can say that money is a crucial resource that requires a high level of discipline in its care and management, meaning proper use.

Nickell and Dorsey describe that, the fundamental plan for how money is used in the family is based on a good understanding with the necessary involvement of both the husband and wife as the primary leaders and managers of financial matters in the family.[11] Discipline in financial decision-making is essential in families because the decisions we make today regarding financial expenditure have consequences that will be seen later in life. To achieve financial success in life, it is crucial to learn the habit of seeking, valuing, saving, using within our capabilities, avoiding its temptations, refraining from using it excessively without putting effort into acquiring it, and finally, developing the habit of using it based on a budget for expenditures aimed at meeting essential priorities. It is essential to understand that there is no small or large amount of money because every amount of money has significant and worthy value according to its appropriate use.

An important point to emphasize about this resource is that every parent/guardian, when providing money to a child, should place great emphasis on the purpose of the money provided. Every parent should tell their child that obtaining any legal money

10. Gabriela, *Importance of Money*, 420.

11. Nickell & Dorsey, *Management in Family Living*, 226.

requires significant and deliberate effort that takes the mind, strength, and time. When it is obtained, it must be respected in its use. This emphasis will help reduce many complaints from many parents about their children's misuse of the money they provide, including school fees.

Therefore, by following these approaches, we can have discipline in the use of money as a crucial resource in the family, and ultimately, we can witness significant financial success in the family because money is the foundation of the success of all developmental activities in the family.

LAND RESOURCES

According to HAKIARDHI, the Land Rights Research and Resources Institute, legally, land resources include everything above and below the surface of the land, including houses, permanent structures, natural vegetation, and all developments except minerals and oil and gas products. These properties are owned by the government or individuals and companies that enter into contracts to exploit them for the benefit of all citizens.[12] Due to these explanations, land plays a significant role in human life and even in the life and development of animals, plants, and all living beings. According to Njau, Katemi, Soka and Jullu, land is a resource needed to develop other sectors of the economy, including industries, commerce, human settlements, agriculture, and other uses. Hence, denying anyone the right to own, use, and maintain land is a violation of human rights.[13]

Due to the increase in population and settlements and the growth in the rate of land use for various purposes such as investment and commercial construction, land has been seen as having great value. Wealthy individuals with resources have been buying and owning large tracts of land, leaving the poor with small plots that are insufficient for their needs. Therefore, due to the growing

---

12. HAKIARDHI, *Masuala Muhimu ya Ardhi*. 1.

13. Njau, Katemi, Soka & Jullu, *Haki za Mwanamke*, 1.

awareness among people in society about the value and importance of land resources, family-owned land must be preserved and developed for the benefit of the entire family generation.

Moreover, it is essential for every family to invest in land because, with the increase in population, settlements, and various other land-related investments, in the future, this resource will become very expensive. Poor families may not be able to own land anymore as it is now. To avoid unnecessary land conflicts in many families, it is crucial for every family to formalize its land ownership according to the law, as doing so not only prevents conflicts but also has benefits in terms of assets, capital, or financial security.

CONCLUSION

Based on the arguments presented by the author in discussing resource management in the family, it is clear that all resources are interdependent in building the well-being of a better family. It is essential to consider each resource as important in building a better family, community, and nation as a whole. This is equivalent to saying that no resource can exist independently without depending on others. However, the foundation of all resources, as discussed, is human resources. It is evident that humans are the leaders and managers of all resources on this planet. The importance of all these resources should be taught to children as soon as they become mentally aware and capable of analyzing various matters, including those related to resources.

DISCUSSION QUESTIONS

(i) Explain what you understand about resources and their importance in the well-being of a family.

(ii) Explain in your perspective the consequences that may arise in a family that does not manage resources adequately.

CHAPTER 5

Styles of Child Upbringing

INTRODUCTION

WHEN DISCUSSING THE STYLES of upbringing, it is essential to ask a fundamental question about the meaning of upbringing. The term upbringing can be interpreted in various ways by different people. For example, in the Arab Knowledge Report, upbringing involves developing a person's self-image, providing the individual with the elements of a social identity, raising awareness, integrating into the cultural and social environment, and preparing for the social and professional roles as an effective and full member of society.[1] According to BAKITA, upbringing means the positive teachings provided by a parent or caregiver in a child's growth, involving instructions on what the child should do and how to do it.[2] Based on these interpretations, upbringing is a sum of teachings a person receives when still young from parents, caregivers, or anyone else in a position to influence the person's life mentally, behaviorally, and ethically. Therefore, according to these definitions, I believe that a person's moral character is rooted in the type of upbringing

1. United Nations Development Programme, *Arab Knowledge Report 2010/2011*, 47.

2. BAKITA, *Kamusi Kuu ya Kiswahili*, 596.

they received as a child. In simpler terms, if a parent fails to raise a child properly, the child, when grown, may engage in inappropriate behaviors in the surrounding society. This truth is emphasized by the experts in parenting and family matters, Uwe, Asuquo and Ekuri who explain that, could parents, who are expected to be the custodians of appropriate behaviour in children be held accountable for such behaviors as a result of their laxity and failure in carrying out their parental responsibilities. Do they in one way or the other contribute to their children's involvement in anti-social practices.[3] Based on Uwe, Asuquo and Ekuri's submission, I suggest that, a parent who does not set clear rules and boundaries for a child can lead the child to develop unacceptable behaviors. The child may end up breaking established laws and, ultimately, find themselves in legal trouble. Hence, this chapter discusses and analyzes the styles of upbringing.

STYLES OF UPBRINGING

Considering the differences in cultures, traditions, and human nature, the issue of upbringing has been a subject of debate about which style of upbringing is suitable for parents to follow. Family and parenting experts such as Smalley; Henggeler, Schoenwald, Borduin, Rowland, and Cunningham; and Mattaini recommend four predominant styles of upbringing, which remain relevant even today.[4][5][6] These styles are categorized into four groups:

1. Upbringing with clear/guiding principles

2. Abusive/Authoritarian upbringing

3. Permissive/Indulgent upbringing

4. Neglectful/Uninvolved upbringing

3. Uwe, Asuquo & Ekuri, *Parenting and Responsibility*, 51.

4. Smalley, *Key to Child's Heart*, 49.

5. Henggeler, Schoenwald, Borduin, Rowland & Cunningham, *Multisystemic Treatment*.

6. Mattaini, *Clinical Intervention with families*.

To fulfill the objectives of this chapter, the discussion will focus on these four styles of upbringing as specified by the experts mentioned above.

UPBRINGING WITH CLEAR/GUIDING PRINCIPLES

Mattaini and Henggeler et al. describe this first type of upbringing as exemplary and worthy of emulation by various parents and caregivers. According to their explanations, various studies have shown that this type of upbringing has resulted in positive outcomes for children.[7] [8] The characteristics of parents/caregivers who believe and live by this type of upbringing include:

i. Parents/caregivers have love and joy, showing no discrimination towards any child in the family.

ii. Parents/caregivers have clear rules with boundaries for all children in the family.

iii. Parents/caregivers allocate time to be with their children, educating them about the family's and society's proper rules and boundaries, and the consequences of violating them.

iv. Parents/caregivers discipline their children after explaining their mistakes and the consequences of their actions, doing so with love.

v. Parents/caregivers are open (communicative) with their children, showing them good things to positively influence them.

vi. When parents/caregivers relax after busy activities, they enjoy playing with their children without favoritism, demonstrating love and happiness towards them.

vii. Parents/caregivers give praise (rewards) to their children for following certain good procedures that uphold acceptable behavior.

---

7. Ibid.

8. Henggeler, et al., *Multi-systemic Treatment.*

viii. Parents/caregivers have a monitoring behavior in upbringing to assist their children. They monitor the child's location, activities, behavior, dreams, and friends.

ix. In one way or another, parents/caregivers ensure that the basic needs of their children are met on time, and their rights are respected by everyone, as explained in Chapter 2.

x. Parents/caregivers avoid spoiling their children by giving them luxury items such as money and other items that show off extravagance.

xi. Parents/caregivers love to teach their children various life skills and techniques based on their abilities, to build their confidence in doing various things as adults.

These are some of the recommended qualities for the current generation to ensure upbringing with clear and appropriate guidelines for the well-being of today and tomorrow's generation. This type of upbringing creates children with the following characteristics:

i. Children who are happy and peaceful at all times.

ii. Children who are mentally independent, emotionally stable, and confident in doing things right, at the right time and place.

iii. Children who respect themselves and others, considering various limits, rules, and existing cultures.

iv. Children who aspire to fulfill their dreams and talents in life.

Thus, all the positive qualities mentioned above that a child, like any other human being, should possess are nurtured by this type of upbringing.

ABUSIVE/AUTHORITARIAN UPBRINGING

According to the perspective of Smalley, this type of upbringing is favored by parents/caregivers with high standards and high expectations for their children in various aspects of their lives, appearing to believe in avoiding mistakes.[9] However, it is important to understand that having high standards and expectations for children in various areas is commendable, but it is wise to believe that due to various reasons, a person may fail to achieve or fulfill a certain thing perfectly. Thus, blaming and possibly punishing a person for not meeting the requirements and expectations of a particular matter without considering the cause or reason that led to not fulfilling the expectations is unwise. Some parents/caregivers have been behind this truth, resorting to using force and abuse to warn their children, thinking it is the right way to raise their children.

Parents/caregivers who embrace this type of upbringing, when asked why they use this system to raise their children, might quickly answer: "You know the today's children are different from us in the past; we should not raise them delicately because they may get used to making mistakes, so we must be very strict when raising them." Many parents/caregivers of this type are those who, in their growing years, were raised harshly by their parents/caregivers. Many young men and women who are seen as morally corrupt today did not start being corrupt today; they started a long time ago as children, and the main reason is the bad upbringing they received from their parents/caregivers. Therefore, parents/caregivers of this type of abusive upbringing have the following characteristics:

i. Parents/caregivers do things that embarrass their children publicly. For example, they like to punish their children even in front of guests. Also, they may dare to punish their children in front of their friends when they visit. Indeed, this is blatant and unacceptable humiliation.

ii. Parents/caregivers have a tendency to show favoritism towards some children, displaying a harsh attitude towards others.

9. Smalley, *Key to Child's Heart*, 49.

However, it is essential for parents/caregivers of this type to be cautious about the Swahili saying that goes, [*mtoto unaye mpende-lea leo kuna dalili za kutokukusaidia kesho na huenda hatafanikiwa kesho kama unayemchukia leo*] "the child you favor today sometimes will not help you tomorrow and may not succeed tomorrow as the one you dislike today."

iii. Parents/caregivers have a habit of comparing their children in terms of excellence/beauty.

For example, they like to say that one is always doing well, and the other is always performing poorly. It is a clear truth that this language is discouraging, as no one does good every day, and no one does bad every day.

iv. Parents/caregivers do not involve their children in various matters but instead force them even in matters affecting their future, such as talents and dreams.

For example, it is common for them to say harshly, "you don't need to know why, just do what I instruct because you shouldn't ask questions or ask me questions, just implement it." Why did you do this? You're senseless, ignorant, and a fool. Today you'll learn; you will recognize me."

The consequences of these statements and similar ones are enough to make a child feel like they are in the middle of fierce animals such as lions, leopards, and bears. With these words, a child may run away from home and live wandering among relatives and acquaintances like a street child or an orphan without parents, hating and resenting their parents' home.

v. Parents do not care about the health and safety of their children, especially when there are signs of danger. In such situations, their language is like this: "Leave it; it will know itself. Leave it to get into trouble; it won't die. It's the problem of its own; it has asked for it, it will stop arguing, and when it comes back, it will recognize who I am."

Certainly, these words and others like them have no signs of liberation or healing for the child; instead, it is enough to say that they have all the signs of killing the child.

vi. Parents/caregivers use very harsh punishment to discipline their children, even without any sign of instruction during punishment.

This is contrary to the Child Law of Tanzania in 2009, as interpreted by Chama cha Wana sheria Tanzania Bara [Tanganyika Law Society], which prohibits severe punishment for children.[10]

vii. Parents do not praise or motivate their children, even if the children have shown great ability and proficiency in a particular matter.

Parents of this type have mouths full of discouraging words, breaking the spirit entirely. When parents return home from work, children scatter, each hiding in their own corner, fearing to be accused of mistakes by parents, even if they feel they haven't committed any. For parents of this type, when they come home, sadness and silence dominate the atmosphere for the children.

viii. Parents/caregivers use harsh, difficult, and heart-wrenching words to the child's heart.

Parents/caregivers speak any words without considering what psychological harm it may cause to the child.

Listen to this true story that I witnessed myself with a parent in a certain region in Tanzania.

In a certain village, there was a single male parent (father) who had lost his wife. His wife passed away, leaving behind four children, with the youngest being just a few months old, not yet reaching the age of one. The infant was raised by the family of the deceased mother because the other children were attending

10. Chama cha Wana sheria Tanzania Bara, *Mtoto na Haki Zake*, 6.

primary school and were still young, requiring care. However, this father was known to be strict with his children, and he had shown this strictness to their mother (deceased) as well, as it was common for him to physically abuse her.

Two years later, this widowed father remarried another woman from a nearby village. After marrying the new wife, he was successful in having more children with her. Fortunately, the child who was left by the deceased mother as an infant grew up and reached the age to attend school. One day, the sixth-grade girl told her father about the need for notebooks and other school supplies. Unfortunately, her father responded harshly and hurtfully, saying, "Get away from me, you big fool, do you have money? Don't bother me, or go ask your mother, over there...". He pointed to where her late mother was buried. With these words, especially pointing to where her mother was buried, the girl cried bitterly in deep pain.

However, the father showed no concern or remorse for his words but continued to chase the girl away, accusing her of making noise. After that, the girl could not continue her studies properly, and she hated her father so much that she did not even want to look him in the eyes. She refused any help from her father and left the house to live where she was raised from a very young age, that is, where her late mother gave birth to her. However, despite being advised to forgive her father, the girl still believes to this day that her father may have been involved in her mother's death.

Due to this story, it is crucial to understand that verbal punishment is more severe than physical punishment for a child because any word spoken by a parent/caretaker lingers. Moreover, words are easily remembered in a child's mind, considering that a mentally sound child has a significant capacity for memorizing and retaining things, especially those that deeply affect or sadden them.

These characteristics and similar ones have significant impacts on a child's upbringing. Examples of negative effects that children raised in this style of parenting may experience include:

i. Children become immune, meaning they are not afraid of punishment because they see it as a part of their lives.

ii. Children develop hardened hearts and a bad spirit in their lives even into adulthood. In simpler terms, these children grow to be merciless individuals in their lives.

iii. Instead of being attracted to good things, children are drawn to negative things that break the ordinary rules of the society they live in.

iv. Due to living in a discouraging environment, children face the problem of lacking self-confidence in their lives. In simple terms, children of this type are filled with fear and a discipline of fear in their lives.

v. Children face the problem of living without goals because they lack certainty about various decisions they can make.

vi. Children inherit the behavior of harshness and cruelty from their parents/guardians and find themselves perpetuating this behavior even when they become parents and guardians themselves.

These and other effects are detrimental to the child, the family, and the nation as a whole. Since today's child is the parent/caretaker and leader of tomorrow, I can say that this style of parenting may be the cause of a society and nation of people without goals, cruel, selfish, and unconcerned about the future of other people's lives. Therefore, due to these effects, it is essential for parents and guardians to avoid this style of parenting as it has no positive outcomes for the child, family, and the nation as a whole. This style of parenting creates a family, community, and nation of people who do not love or respect each other. Additionally, this style of parenting contributes significantly to the increase of street children and those living in risky environments.

PERMISSIVE/INDULGENT UPBRINGING

Many parents and guardians fail to differentiate between genuinely loving a child (true friendship) and spoiling a child. Thus, they unknowingly give their children excessive freedom before they develop the ability to think, reason, and make decisions independently. This style of parenting is implemented by parents and guardians from families considered wealthy or those who have held onto their wealth for a long time without having children or those with only one child. Smalley describe that environments like these may allow children to do whatever they want. Parents and guardians who value this style of parenting have the following characteristics:[11]

i. Parents/guardians of this parenting style tend to have an encouraging but weak approach in setting rules and boundaries for their children.

ii. Parents/guardians have the habit of giving their children luxury items and pleasures such as money, phones, cars, etc., even before they can handle them responsibly. It should be noted that these items are not inherently bad, but if owned improperly and at an inappropriate age, they can become toxic in the overall development of the child.

iii. Parents/guardians do not like punishing their children when they make mistakes. Instead, they end up saying things like "you....!, don't do that, it's wrong," appearing not to take what they say seriously.

iv. Parents/guardians have the habit of defending their children even when they seem to mistreat other children or break the law.

For example, these parents tend to defend their children, especially when they are seen being expelled from school, claiming that their children have been mistreated by teachers.

11. Smalley, *Key to Child's Heart*, 49.

Listen to this true story involving my student and her parent in a certain region here in Tanzania.

I had a female student in certain school who was the only daughter to her parents. This girl was dearly loved by her parents. Her biological father was a political leader and a well-known figure in the village where they lived. Due to the influence he had, he was among the members of the school board.

Due to the way this girl was babied and not properly disciplined by her parents, she engaged in prostitution to a significant extent. Her appearance and physical attributes attracted many boys in the school, and she engaged in sexual activities with them, including some teachers who failed to uphold ethical teaching standards.

One day, this girl, along with a group of other girls with similar behavior, escaped from the dormitory on a Sunday afternoon and went to a nearby bush. On that day, they secretly sought a local photographer through fellow non-resident students. In that bush, they took pictures in various poses, wearing only their undergarments. Fortunately, the school administration received information about this shameful incident through the matron, school guards, and some good Samaritan neighbors.

The school administration, a few days later, conducted an unannounced inspection by entering the girls' dormitory to check beds and luggage, led by female teachers. In this surprise inspection, they discovered these explicit photos in the bags of the girls involved in the scandal.

After summoning these girls and questioning them, they admitted to the incident. According to the school rules, these girls were supposed to be expelled to prevent them from influencing other students negatively. Before their expulsion, their parents were called to the school by the administration to be informed about the incident and then take their children at home.

The surprising thing is that the parent who was a political leader, a prominent figure, and a school board member, among all the other parents, alone denied that their child was involved in the incident. The parent went further to claim that the incident was orchestrated and that it was a plot carried out by teachers harboring personal grudges against his child, collaborating with students, to entrap his child unknowingly in order to have her expelled from school.

That parent insisted that his child has good behavior and has been unfairly treated. Due to his political and social standing as a prominent figure, he vowed to ensure legal action against the school administration and even escalate the matter to the ministry, alleging that his child is being victimized and should not be expelled from school.

This matter caused significant turmoil to the extent that the school owners requested the district government, through the education officer, to intervene in order to provide legal guidance on school management and the administration of disciplinary measures for students.

In reaching a consensus, the government leadership through the education officer stated that based on evidence and disciplinary procedures, the girl along with her peers is legitimately expelled from the school. Furthermore, that parent along with other parents were advised to transfer their children to schools located far from that area.

What do you learn from this incident? Reflect deeply, oh parent.

v. Parents love to give their children everything they see as good in their eyes, even if it comes at a high cost. This removes the children's tendency to be content and satisfied with what they have.

vi. Parents do not hesitate to accompany their children to entertainment venues or sit together watching morally inappropriate films and videos. For example, romantic films or going with them to questionable places.

vii. Parents grant their children the freedom to go anywhere, anytime, which makes them feel free to engage in inappropriate activities such as early romantic relationships, etc.

viii. Parents allow children the freedom to choose and wear clothes they claim to like, following current fashion trends, even if they reveal intimate body parts contrary to our societal morals.

There is no doubt that with this type of upbringing, we cannot have a better and morally upright family, as it is an undeniable truth that parents serve as mirrors and wellsprings of morality for today's children, who are tomorrow's parents and the nation of today and tomorrow. Such upbringing has the following effects on children:

i. Children find themselves engaging in immoral activities at a young age due to excessive freedom.

ii. Due to lack of control, children sometimes find themselves in risky environments.

iii. Children raised in this way always see themselves as superior to others and as rulers who can control others as they wish.

iv. Children raised in this manner are highly likely to struggle to do many things on their own without the assistance of others.

In simple terms, these children tend to have a dependent mindset, which makes their lives challenging once they leave their parents' homes and start new lives; for example, when they get married.

v. Children from such upbringing lack the ability to cope with difficult situations when they arise.

vi. Children raised this way tend to be lazy in thinking and are unwilling to engage in productive activities.

vii. Children of this upbringing lack the habit of showing respect to their peers or those older than them. Similarly, they do not have the habit of humility, especially when there are differences with those older than them.

In simple terms, they are children with a tendency to disdain others.

viii. Children of this upbringing have unrestricted humor, both towards their parents, guardians, and other people, which can create obstacles for some individuals.

These are some of the effects resulting from this style of upbringing. Based on the information provided about this upbringing and its effects, it can be said that a generation with poor morals and a deficiency in self-thinking, emotional self-control, and intellectual independence is a specific outcome of this type of upbringing. Therefore, parents and guardians should learn to raise their children by considering moderation and limits in every aspect. Children always need guidance from parents/guardians with love, following the principles of good ethical upbringing. Parents, guardians, and teachers should not deny children discipline or any other form of punishment, as long as it is moderate, while explaining the reasons and benefits of the discipline before implementing it with love.

NEGLECTFUL/UNINVOLVED UPBRINGING

The joy of a child is always to be in the presence of both parents, as every child is the product of both parents. Therefore, the closeness of parents to the child is essential for the child's well-being in every aspect of life from childhood to adulthood. However, as Gangel pointed out in his perspective on neglectful upbringing, there are various reasons why children are abandoned. These reasons still seem to have a strong influence in many parts of the world today. Some of these reasons include:[12]

---

12. Gangel, *The Family First.*

(i) High Divorce Rates

According to Mwanahiza, divorce has become a common occurrence in this era of globalization, leading to various consequences in families.[13] The most affected by divorce are usually the children. The significant impact children experience is the loss of the close and shared love between both parents, i.e., the father and mother. Eventually, children find themselves divided as if they were commodities, with some taken by one parent and others by the other parent, or all being left with one parent. Not only that, there are times when each parent neglects the children, leading to some children living on the streets and facing various problems.

According to Malunde, a report released by the Shinyanga Paralegal Aid Centre (PACESH) in Shinyanga region in Tanzania on September 29, 2021, states that marital conflicts (separation/divorce) are still a cause of child abuse incidents, leading to children taking on family responsibilities and contributing to school dropout, teenage pregnancies and marriages, and the wandering of children when their parents separate.[14] Thus, based on these explanations, it is evident that divorce is one of the sources of neglectful upbringing.

(ii) Increase of Working Mothers

In the history of many societies worldwide, women were seen as having the primary responsibility of staying close to children while engaging in various household tasks that kept them close to their children. Unlike in the past, nowadays, mothers have also entered the workforce, just like men.

Mwanahiza explains that approximately three decades have passed since we achieved the advancements in science and technology that have been a catalyst for revolutions in our families and society as a whole.[15] These changes have significantly affected our families in terms of upbringing, causing both fathers and mothers

13. Mwanahiza, *Utandawazi na Malezi*, para. 9.

14. Malunde, *Migogoro ya Ndoa*, para. 1.

15. Mwanahiza, *Utandawazi na Malezi*, para. 8.

to leave their young children and work in offices away from home all day, leaving the children with other caregivers. Previously, the woman was the primary family caregiver while the man left home to provide for the family. The shift of both parents working away from their families has led to a decline in morals for children. However, we need to ask ourselves, is it wrong for mothers to enter the job market just like men? In my view, it is not wrong, and I see it as a misguided concept that denies women the opportunity to showcase their talents equally with men.

What I believe is that the issue of busyness in work matters is inevitable for both women and men in this globalized world, as it is one of the characteristics of globalization. Many parents have found themselves lacking time to be close to their children to provide them with proper upbringing. For example, there are many parents who leave early in the morning while their children are still asleep, and when they return in the evening from work, they find their children already asleep. Sometimes, when they return, they continue with office work, which does not give them time to spend with their children.

Listen to this true story that happened in a certain region in Tanzania:

One parent, my friend and a government official, once told me that he has a lot of responsibilities at his office. He mentioned that on weekdays, from Monday to Friday, he leaves home early in the morning to go to his office and returns home late at night. He leaves his children sleeping, and by the time he returns, they are already asleep.

One weekend, while he was taking a break, his younger child asked him a question, "Dad, where do you live these days, and when did you come? Why do we always live with mom, and you are not around?" This friend of mine was troubled by this question. He then answered the child, saying that he is always there but has a lot of work at the office, which sometimes keeps him away. The child asked the parent a challenging question, "Dad, *do you love work more than us?" The parent replied to the child, expressing that he loves them more than work, which is why he goes to work early and returns late to ensure they have all their needs. The child laughed and said, "Okay, Dad."*

These questions made this parent request a reduction in responsibilities at work so that his workload would decrease, allowing him more time to spend with his children, assisting their mother in upbringing.

This story teaches us that, based on the reasons provided by Gangel and the explanations by Mwanahiza, it's not only women who are busy with job responsibilities that can lead to neglectful parenting, but also men, due to the busy nature of their employment, can contribute to neglectful parenting. Therefore, I urge both male and female parents, despite their busy work schedules, to make an effort to set aside time to spend with their children to teach them essential values and ethics.

(iii) Excessive Television Watching

Watching television is not inherently bad, as it allows us to learn and be guided in our daily lives. However, excessive television watching has had significant negative effects on families and society as a whole. Nowadays, many parents, when returning from work, spend a considerable amount of their break time watching television instead of utilizing that time to be with their children and impart essential parenting advice. Therefore, if parents and caregivers cannot exercise moderation and prioritize important matters over television watching, this situation can contribute significantly to neglectful parenting.

(iv) Increase in Computer Usage

In many developed countries, the lifestyle is heavily influenced by computer systems. Due to the uniqueness of this device, individuals with literacy skills find themselves spending extended periods on computers, sometimes neglecting other responsibilities. Some use this time for developmental activities, while others engage in various forms of entertainment, including popularly known 'Games.' This phenomenon affects both male and female parents and caregivers, leading them to spend more time on computers than with their children, teaching them crucial values.

(v) Increased Mobility in Society

There are various reasons for people relocating from one place to another, such as seeking better economic opportunities, jobs, or fertile land for agriculture. Additionally, some move to escape conflicts and seek safety due to disputes or wars between communities or nations. These reasons have led many parents and caregivers to move away from their children, either intentionally for economic reasons or unintentionally due to safety concerns. Consequently, these factors have resulted in many children growing up without their parents, being raised by relatives, friends, or various aid organizations.

(vi) Dependence on and Trust in Domestic Workers, Commonly Known as Housemaids and Houseboys

In recent years, after women entered the job market similarly to men, a trend of hiring domestic workers to help with childcare emerged. These domestic workers have played a significant role in the upbringing of working parents' children. While they have assisted many working parents in preparing and taking their children to school, as well as providing care in their absence, some parents have become overly reliant on these workers, neglecting their responsibility to spend quality time with their children and teach them essential values.

(vii) Surge in the Use of Social Media

With the rapid advancement of information and communication technology, the world has witnessed a significant shift in the media landscape. This transformation has led to the emergence of various social media platforms like Facebook, Twitter, YouTube, Instagram, WhatsApp, TikTok, and others. However, the rapid adoption of social media has resulted in many parents spending more time chatting and communicating with colleagues or friends online than being physically present with their children, providing them with essential guidance. This lack of closeness due to excessive use of social media has become one of the causes of neglectful parenting.

Moreover, this situation has sometimes caused harm to very young children, such as poisoning, burns, or falls from high places, leading to tragic consequences due to inadequate supervision from parents. Listen to this story from various media outlets in Romania Ayo reports.[16]

Two twin children have died after falling from the tenth floor while their mother was entertaining herself live on Facebook. The twins met their demise after climbing through an open window. The incident occurred in the city of Ploiesti in Romania.

Police report that the mother of the children did not realize that her kids had fallen and died until she heard the sound of ambulance sirens and someone knocking on her door. Throughout this time, she was live on Facebook, conversing with her followers on her page. It has been explained that Andreea Violeta Petrice, the mother, forgot to close the window that the children used to play and attempt to exit, leading to their fatal fall.

After opening the door for the person knocking, she was informed that the twin children had fallen and passed away. The mother quickly went to her children's room to check if they were hers, only to discover they were not there, and the window was left open.

Therefore, by highlighting this truly saddening incident, I advise parents/guardians to reduce the time spent chatting on social media, especially when they are responsible for ensuring the safety

16. Ayo, *Watoto Waporomoka Ghorofani.*

of young children. Moreover, it is advisable that they spend more time with their children to ensure their safety and teach them various aspects of upbringing. These reasons and others, in general, suffice to introduce us to the type of parents who cherish this kind of parenting, which seems neglectful and abandoning of children in the entire realm of upbringing, especially in this era of globalization. This style of parenting has significant effects on children. Some of these effects include:

    i. Children grow up with an upbringing lacking proper ethics and various life skills from their parents.

    ii. Children lead a wandering life without a clear direction.

    iii. Children are raised in a way that they cannot perform tasks with perfection.

    iv. Children lack an understanding of the value of a parent.

Therefore, this style of parenting should not be followed by parents or guardians in raising children if they genuinely expect to have morally upright children that reflect the behavior and ethics of those parents.

CONCLUSION

In general, I can say that this chapter has discussed very crucial aspects in this book as it attempts to unravel a very challenging puzzle, especially in today's times, regarding which style of parenting is suitable for raising children in a family. This chapter focuses on parents and guardians regarding their parenting qualities and how they themselves can contribute to building or destroying their generations, rather than blaming external factors such as globalization for allegedly corrupting the morals of their children.

DISCUSSION QUESTIONS:

i. Provide your advice on what should be done to maintain the type of parenting you have identified as the best.

ii. Divorce, as discussed in this book, appears to be one of the causes of neglectful parenting, but the government recognizes and accepts it when one parent sees no reason to continue living with the other, regardless of having children together. Explain your perspective considering the effects of divorce on children and the legality of divorce.

CHAPTER 6

Concept of Globalization

INTRODUCTION

IN THIS CHAPTER, THE author illustrates how the term globalization has dominated all areas of relationships in today's world. It is evident that globalization has become a topic of discussion in various fields such as social, cultural, educational, political, economic, and technological. As this term has gained widespread popularity and is seen as a subject of debate, it is essential to examine its context. The objectives of this chapter are to explain the historical concept of globalization, demonstrate globalization within families, discuss the temptations of children in the era of globalization and how parents are responsible for meeting and controlling those temptations, and examine the advantages and disadvantages of globalization in upbringing.

To achieve the outlined objectives, this chapter covers the following aspects: various perspectives on the meaning of globalization, the history of globalization and its global spread, the state of globalization within families, various factors that constitute children's desires, especially in the current era of globalization, how parents are responsible for controlling those desires, and the significance of globalization despite being perceived as a source of ethical erosion for children and youth in many families.

MEANING OF GLOBALIZATION

Since globalization is a debatable term, it must be examined from various perspectives. For instance, Mwangosi in his exposition based on Sullivan and Chachage perspective, explains that globalization is a concept aimed at reducing or eliminating the authority of the state in a country by increasing the authority of international organizations to control the capabilities of national organizations.[1] Mwangosi further emphasizes that globalization intends to remove geographical and political barriers to allow the free flow of labor between nations.[2] On the other hand, globalization is a concept used to describe cultural, economic, educational, and political interactions that surpass and cross the boundaries of one nation to another, disseminated through ideologies, technology, and language.

According to Mbonde, globalization is an extensive expansion and spread of deep-seated relationships among different societies concerning various aspects of life, from societal well-being to survival activities, economic, cultural, defense, trade, investment, communication, and technology. This economic and cultural globalization has positioned the United States at a rapid pace in controlling and influencing these transformations.[3] Reflecting in Rugumamu, Mbonde states: "In general terms, the concept of globalization means making the whole world appear as one village by expanding communication, social, and economic relations in various aspects such as economy, culture, business, investment, technology, and even spiritually."[4] Based on this understanding, it is claimed that the world's economy is in the process of

1. Mwangosi, *Riwaya ya Babu Alipofufuka*, 125.
2. *Ibid.* 125.
3. Mbonde, *Methali za Kiutandawazi*, 9.
4. *Ibid.* 10.

integration, breaking down borders and consolidating operating forces into one entity.

Given these perspectives as described above, it is clear that the concept of globalization is extensive, depending on people's viewpoints. Therefore, globalization is a process that makes the whole world appear as a cooperative association with diverse members having different thoughts, forced to build relationships in various areas such as cultures, education, business, economy, politics, and technology.

However, in my perspective, there are signs that, once reached, this association might lead to a single leader for the entire world, a single currency, a single identity, or even a single belief system. Therefore, individuals, families, and society as a whole cannot escape this system and must consider it as an integral part of child rearing and life in general in today's society. The fundamental question for individuals, families, and society as a whole is, "How can we continue to raise the current generation on ethical foundations while respecting our traditions, customs, and cultures alongside the demands of globalization?"

HISTORY OF GLOBALIZATION

In discussing the history of globalization, there is a significant divergence of perspectives among scholars and analysts of historical issues worldwide. Some write about the history and emergence of globalization, focusing solely on the growth of science and technology, which is one component of the entire concept of globalization. For example, Mbonde describes the history of globalization, stating, "The concept of globalization emerged in the late 1980s, thrived in the 1990s, and became a challenge in various fields."[5] According to Mbonde's explanation, it is clear that globalization is a relatively new concept, a notion I disagree with because the late 1980s and early 1990s were periods when technological growth began to manifest, especially in developing countries.

5. *Ibid.* 9.

The manifestation of technological growth cannot be considered the sole beginning of globalization but rather the beginning of the expansion of the concept of globalization and not its actual commencement.

It is important to note that the history of globalization is carried by relationships that cross traditional, cultural, economic, political, technological, and commercial borders from one country to another and from one continent to another. Thus, globalization is not a new concept, as some people, scholars, and historical analysts believe. What I believe about global relationships is that they began when the first humans began to interact culturally, even though records of these cultural relationship journeys were not written in history books as they are today.

According to Toussaint, relationships become evident, especially when the world witnessed what is now called the discovery of the New World, North and South America, by the Italian navigator Christopher Columbus in 1492. Additionally, in Africa and Asia, these relationships become noticeable in the 15th century when Europeans, led by explorers and traders from Portugal such as Bartolomeu Dias (1488) and Vasco da Gama (1498), discovered the continents of Africa and Asia.[6]

Due to the discovery of the Americas by Christopher Columbus from Europe, trade, economic, and cultural relationships between Europe and America began, marking the clear beginning of the concept of globalization in that region. Similarly, due to the alleged discovery of Africa and Asia by Bartolomeu Dias and Vasco da Gama from Europe, these relationships were led by the Portuguese, Dutch, English, and French who established trading posts. During that time, the slave trade, managed by Arabs and some Africans themselves, continued to grow rapidly, becoming a significant force and marking the clear beginning of the concept of globalization in this region.

These relationships continued to grow from century to century since the 15th century when they became explicitly evident until the 19th century when they were further propelled by the

6. Toussaint, *Globalization from Christopher Columbus.*

rapid growth of information and communication technology to this day, where the world continues to be interconnected in all areas, making it resemble a small village. Mrikaria emphasizes this by stating that, on the other hand, these changes in new communication technology have made the world smaller and smaller every day.[7] Hence, when I look at the history of globalization in general, I see a fusion of various cultures globally, which are the foundation of upbringing in families. These cultures differ in various aspects related to traditions and customs, which are the pillars in the construction of our families.

Therefore, the history of globalization shows us that as changes continue to emerge in the entire lifestyle system, especially due to the interaction of cultures, reflecting on the issue of upbringing in our societies becomes crucial. From the discussion built in this section, it is evident that globalization is not a new concept; it began a long time ago, especially when humans started to culturally relate.

GLOBALIZATION IN THE FAMILY

In today's world, the term globalization has taken center stage in various aspects, especially when discussing the ethics of children and youth. If globalization were a person, it would likely live under significant stress due to the numerous accusations directed at it, blaming it for the erosion of morals in children and youth within families. This is because globalization, to a large extent, appears to have significant negative effects, particularly in terms of ethics, which many families struggle to control.

Globalization has transformed the world and everything within it, including families, into a fast-moving entity, like a ship sailing too fast and unable to maintain its specific course due to intense waves from all sides of the ocean. Accidents causing significant harm, such as injuries and deaths, have become common and unavoidable. In the past, during times of communal living, human

7. Mrikaria, *Fasihi Simulizi na Teknolojia*, 201.

communities could resist and overcome various environmental, political, economic, social, and cultural changes. However, today's changes are more scientific and technological. Indeed, modern societies are changing societies. In such contemporary societies, "the proportion of change that is either planned or issues from the secondary consequences of deliberate innovations is much higher than in former times.[8] In fact, human needs and passions change over time, influenced by research and development, the discovery of new machines, the creation of new sources of power, and the continuous development of new methods to meet these needs. Hence, all of these factors stimulate new passions and desires among humans.

Additionally, as these changes occur, people invent and adopt new rules, new devices, and new products in the technological environment faster than they can adapt to changes in their personal lives. Unfortunately, the overall human environment has become challenging to control.

The effects of these changes on individuals and their various institutions, including families as essential human institutions, have led to conflicts. Humans continually create and receive new procedures, new equipment, and new products in the technological environment faster than they can accept changes in their personal lives. These changes fuel conflicts and new desires, especially among youth.

As globalization seems to enter and settle in families, the question to ask is, should we run away from it? If we run away, where should we run to avoid it? Since globalization is perceived as a significant adversary that has already invaded families, fleeing might not be the right solution. Running away from a problem is never the proper way to address the problem itself; instead, it's about facing it. Furthermore, because the world is full of challenges, there is no place to escape globalization; we will encounter it wherever we go.

Therefore, we must understand globalization and all its characteristics as a potential adversary to the family. We need to know

8. Rajan, Process of Social Change, 5.

how to confront it using our weapons: our traditions, customs, and cultures; our environment and our technology. We cannot avoid globalization and its consequences if we do not seek to understand it more and comprehend how to avoid its negative effects while embracing and appreciating its positive impacts.

RESPONSIBILITIES OF PARENTS AND THE DESIRES OF CHILDREN IN THE ERA OF GLOBALIZATION

In these times of rapid globalization, children are attracted to many things more than in the past. Similarly, the way parents should meet the desires of children regarding various attractions is entirely different from what it used to be. Ngugi explains that children have great enthusiasm for their surroundings, especially regarding animals, birds, and other things. If we do not consider the various enthusiasms of children, we will end up suppressing or killing their enthusiasm, thus breaking their motivation to learn.[9] Therefore, it is true that there are many things that children desire to have, see, and engage with.

In this section, I will disclose things that are part of children's desires, especially in the era of globalization:

i. The desire to be loved and listened to,

ii. The desire for food,

iii The desire for clothing,

iv. The desire to visit attractive places,

v. The desire to visit relatives in big cities,

vi. The desire to own communication devices,

vii. The desire to attend sports and entertainment events,

viii. The desire to build friendships,

ix. The desire to attend good schools.

9. Ngugi, *Fasihi ya Wototo*, 173–74.

THE DESIRE TO BE LOVED AND LISTENED TO

Any sane human being needs to be loved and feel heard when expressing their feelings about something. If a person is deprived of love and the opportunity to be heard, they are at risk of experiencing stress, which can make them feel worthless and unfit to live on this planet. According to Mjingwa, Pope Francis Angelus, the leader of the Catholic Church, says that everyone needs the oil of comfort, love, and careful service! ... to receive the "Holy Anointing" of being listened to, loved, good neighborliness, and careful service.[10] Being loved goes hand in hand with being listened to, and these are the desires of all human beings, both young and old. However, this desire is crucial for young children, especially in this era of globalization, where acts of violence are increasing in global societies, especially against young children who cannot defend themselves like adults.

In the Holy Bible, specifically in the Song of Solomon chapter 8, verses 6–7, King Solomon writes: "6 Place me like a seal over your heart, like a seal on your arm; for love is as strong as death, its jealousy unyielding as the grave. It burns like blazing fire, like a mighty flame. 7 Many waters cannot quench love; rivers cannot sweep it away. If one were to give all the wealth of one's house for love, it would be utterly scorned." Examining this quote from the Holy Bible, it is evident that the power within love is compared to the strength of death. This could imply that if a person lacks love and is not listened to, the alternative might be death. This is a truth that becomes evident when considering various cases of people who committed suicide or sought revenge due to a lack of love and being heard. While these incidents often occur in adults, young children who lack love find themselves seeking it outside the family. The consequence is that many end up running away from home and living with relatives, neighbors, friends, or even getting married at a young age.

Consider this real-life story of a student in a certain region of Tanzania:

10. Mjingwa, *Papa Francisko*, para. 4.

80

One female student from a certain primary school, who was in fifth grade, lacked the attention of her parents. This student came from a wealthy family and attended a prestigious school with ample resources. In her bedroom at home, she had various luxuries such as a computer, television, phone, and other items that could bring her joy, just like any other child. Unfortunately, she attended a school that was very far from her home. She was the first to be picked up by the school bus early in the morning and the last to be dropped off late in the evening. The school bus had a driver and a conductor known to the students as 'uncle,' a term commonly used for bus drivers and conductors in Tanzania.

Unfortunately, these 'uncles' were not good people; they subjected her to cruel acts and threatened her not to speak to her parents or teachers about it. The driver would rape her every morning when she was picked up, considering she was the first to board the bus, and the conductor would rape her in the evening when others were getting off since she was the last to disembark daily.

Regrettably, whenever this child returned home and tried to be close to her parents to explain what she went through every day on her way to and from school, they refused to listen. These parents were harsh, telling her to go to her room and not stay in the living room, encouraging her to study in her room and find solace there because they had provided everything she needed. For several months, she had no opportunity to sit with her parents and explain her suffering. Additionally, even at school, she couldn't find a teacher she could confide in, given the threats from the 'uncles' not to speak to parents or teachers.

One day, social workers from an organization dealing with child protection visited the school as part of their project to address children's issues. While interviewing children about their likes and dislikes and providing questionnaires, this particular child responded differently. She said, "I don't like the distance from home to school, and from school to home. I don't like the school 'uncles,' I don't like school, I don't like home, I don't like dad or mom, but I like my sister, our house girl, a little bit." These answers were markedly different from those of other children and caught the attention of the professionals, who decided to call her and inquire more deeply about her responses.

The child explained why she disliked everything she had rejected, and the main reason was the lack of close love and not being listened to by her parents regarding the actions of the school bus 'uncles.' She felt that the only person who listened to her was the house girl, but unfortunately, her parents had warned her not to confide in the house girl about her private matters, saying she wasn't a family member and was transient.

After speaking with the professionals, they requested the school administration to summon her biological mother, who then came. Upon hearing the challenges her daughter faced, the mother collapsed, fainting in anguish over the issues her child had been enduring for months. When she regained consciousness, she apologized to her daughter. Fortunately, the child was found not to have contracted any diseases. She continued to receive psychological support to return to a state of happiness and feel free at home and school.

This story is very saddening. Parents, caregivers, and teachers have a very significant responsibility to be close to our children while showing them love and listening to them. A child's first friend is their parent or caregiver or anyone close to them with the aim of providing good upbringing, such as a teacher or a religious leader. If we fail to show them love, listen to them, and bring them close, we will miss out on knowing many good and bad things they encounter. As a result, they may find themselves deteriorating slowly, and we will only come to know that they have deteriorated by seeing the consequences when it's too late to help. The proverbs;

"prevention is better than cure" and *"once water is spilled, it cannot be scooped up again"* should remind us of our significant duty to love and listen to our children, especially in this era of globalization where the challenges children face are numerous, both in the community, at home, and in school.

FOOD PREFERENCES

Food is always the closest and primary companion for every living being, whether human, animal, insect, or plant. This is because no creature can survive without food. According to the perspective of Ashakiran and Deepthi, we eat food to maintain health, which is essential for the sustainable life of living beings.[11] Unfortunately, changes in lifestyle have led us to overlook careful consideration of the style of food necessary for good health.

In describing the concept of lifestyle changes and healthy nutrition, Ashakiran and Deepthi explain that globalization and urbanization have greatly affected one's eating habits and forced many people to consume fancy and high calorie fast foods, popularly known as 'Junk foods'. Junk food simply means an empty calorie food. An empty calorie food is a high calorie or calorie rich food which lacks in micronutrients such as vitamins, minerals, or amino acids, and fiber but has high energy (calories). These foods don't contain the nutrients that your body needs to stay healthy. Hence, these foods that has poor nutritional value is considered unhealthy and may be called as junk food.[12] Unfortunately, scientific research indicates that such foods have significant adverse effects on our bodies, leading to diseases such as diabetes, hypertension, and heart conditions.[13] Regrettably, these are the types of foods that children often prefer.

Referring to Zhu and colleagues, Ashakiran and Deepthi discuss a study conducted in Beijing, China, which revealed that the

11. Ashakiran & Deepthi, *Fast Foods*, 7.

12. *Ibid.* 7.

13. *Ibid.* 7.

consumption of fast foods is prevalent among young children and adolescents aged between 8 and 16. This type of dietary habit not only affects their physical growth but also influences their focus, diligence, emotions, and behavior. The study also found that many mothers significantly prefer feeding their children fast foods over natural foods, even though natural foods have fewer negative impacts on their health and cognitive development.[14] Consequently, parents play a crucial role in controlling the consumption of fast foods, which are often seen as luxurious and appealing to today's children.

To control the excessive consumption of such foods, my perspective is that parents should encourage their children to adopt a more natural food-oriented diet. It's essential to explain the benefits of consuming natural foods and the drawbacks of relying too much on modern, processed foods. However, I am not suggesting that children should be completely deprived of modern foods, as there are behavioral consequences, especially when they are denied such foods for an extended period at home, only to encounter them in restaurants, hotels, events, entertainment venues, or neighbors' homes.

For instance, in our current society, many children have been tempted to engage in unethical activities, including promiscuity, with the promise of being provided with modern foods such as fried potatoes (commonly known as chips), roasted meat, etc. To prevent children from perceiving these foods as extremely significant and exotic compared to natural foods, it is crucial for parents to prepare these foods themselves at home. Moreover, it is essential to ensure that children receive good, sufficient, and timely meals.

CLOTHING PREFERENCES

Due to significant lifestyle changes in our society, largely driven by globalization, the issue of various fashion styles has rapidly grown and intensified competition in the clothing industry, especially for children and youth. Consequently, clothing serves as a significant

14. *Ibid.* 11.

attraction or desire for children. While emphasizing the importance of clothing as a significant desire for children, Johansson explains that clothing holds great importance in various uses for children, especially those approaching adolescence. Some clothing items serve as decorations and attractions more than others.[15]

Regarding being drawn to a particular type of clothing, children are often influenced by a certain fashion when they see their peers wearing it. Mohtar and Abbas confirm that matured children influence each other when they imitate or establish a certain lifestyle trend.[16] Therefore, based on Mohtar and Abbas's explanations, it is evident that clothing desires, especially for new styles, are significantly influenced by seeing or being influenced by their peers.

Hence, I can assert that parents have a significant responsibility to control their children's emotions regarding clothing and new fashion trends. Parents should create a culture of sitting down with their children to explain the positive and negative aspects of clothing, considering the customs and traditions of their community. Nevertheless, parents should also cultivate a culture of going shopping together with their children, allowing them to choose clothes they like while adhering to the teachings about the nature of clothing.

VISITING PLACES WITH ATTRACTIONS (TOURISM)

Walks that take place in areas with various attractions or specific relaxation spots are recognized as tourism. Many people enjoy such walks, although most of them may not be aware that they are engaging in tourism. According to United Nations World Tourism Organization (UNWTO), tourism is a social, cultural, and economic phenomenon that involves people leaving their countries or usual places to go to other places for personal, commercial, or professional purposes. These people are called visitors (which may be either tourists or excursionists; residents or nonresidents) and

15. Johansson, *Doing Age and Gender*, 284.

16. Mohtar & Abbas, *Teenager's Preferences and Choice*, 99.

tourism has to do with their activities, some of which imply tourism expenditure.[17]

The UNWTO's definition of tourism can be divided into two main categories: domestic tourism, which involves walks in residential areas (within the country), and international tourism, which involves walks in areas outside the residence (outside the country).

In general, tourism involves walks in areas with attractions such as beach areas, natural and man-made gardens, historical museum sites, wildlife parks/reserves, and luxurious buildings. These places are widely loved, especially by children, as they have many things that can amaze them and make them play and enjoy life more.

The issue of tourism walks largely appears to be a new and rapidly growing culture among our communities in developing countries, while it seems like a long-standing cultural norm for people in Western countries. Therefore, since this issue of walks seems to be greatly loved and attractive to many people, especially children, it is important for parents to cultivate a culture of having visits to various places with various attractions for children. However, this culture of having sightseeing visits has many benefits for growing children, as it can help them learn and understand many geographical and historical aspects. This culture is one of the cultures that build the whole concept of globalization.

DESIRE TO VISIT RELATIVES IN BIG CITIES

Due to the significant increase in the speed of many children attending school due to government emphasis on achieving education goals for all, many children do not have regular time to visit relatives, especially those in big cities. Then, many children, especially those in school, prefer to travel, especially to big cities, during school breaks to see relatives and family members, as well as to experience a change of environment and learn many things

17. United Nations World Tourism Organization, *Understanding Tourism*, 1.

in those cities. Changing the environment for a certain period is very beneficial for children as it provides them with experience and understanding of many environmental aspects, ultimately eliminating unnecessary naivety. However, it is important to consider the safety of children when allowing them to travel to visit relatives and family.

The Illinois Department of Children and Family Services (IDCFS) defines that the travel and communication plan should indicate the place and time where the travel will take place and a designated person responsible for receiving the child undertaking the trip.[18] These details clearly show that when allowing children to visit relatives, communication and safety must be transparent between the child's origin and the destination of the visit.

Therefore, parents and guardians, as explained in this section, have a significant responsibility when allowing children to undertake such visits, especially in these times when cases of child abduction have been reported in many communities.

DESIRE TO OWN COMMUNICATION DEVICES

Due to the growth of information and communication technology, a major catalyst for globalization, the desire to own communication devices has become significant, especially for children and youth, particularly in developing countries. This is due to the increase in the production of such devices, accompanied by a decrease in prices, especially for devices that are not stable and of high quality. This has led to a strong desire among young people and children to own these devices, such as phones, computers, etc.

Communication devices, especially phones, have become a significant attraction for young children and adolescents, especially those in school. Parents and school teachers have reported many incidents involving children using their parents' devices without close supervision. According to a study conducted by the British Broadcasting Corporation (BBC) in Kaspersky's lab, it was

---

18. Illinois Department of Children and Family Services, *Brothers and Sisters' Connection*, 6.

reported that 18% of interviewed parents in the UK had lost money or data from their phones or tablets because their children were using the parents' devices without close supervision.[19] The report explains that children who have unrestricted access to the internet often purchase games or apps, leading to misuse of money.

However, despite children's personal efforts to own these communication devices, especially phones, the BBC report shows that more than 20% of parents do not closely monitor what their children do online. It also showed that nowadays parents are not aware of the dangers of using the internet on tablets and mobile phones, as they were when the child used a computer.[20]

In this era of globalization dominated by a free market that allows people to do whatever business they want, even if it undermines morals in society, parents have a significant responsibility in controlling young children from using communication devices before they reach an age of self-awareness. In many modern smartphones, popularly known as "Smartphones," there are numerous apps, some of which allow access to explicit content, which poses a significant ethical danger to children in their development.

However, parents should educate children about the importance of using communication devices, especially phones, for the purpose of facilitating communication between individuals. Therefore, it is crucial for children to be guided and supervised on the proper use of phones and other communication devices, especially when it is necessary for communication only.

The advice given by the author in this paragraph aligns with the position taken by participants in the Rome conference held on October 6, 2017, regarding the dignity of young children in the digital world as reported by Mjingwa. In this statement, participants urge various stakeholders in the development of science and communication technology to take responsibility for leading the fight to ensure the protection and safety of children on the internet. Participants encourage families, neighbors, and communities

---

19. British Broadcasting Corporation News Swahili, *Athari za Smartphones*, para. 1.

20. Ibid, para. 3.

from various parts of the world, as well as children themselves, to recognize the potential harm caused by misuse of social media.[21] Therefore, all advice should be carefully considered to ensure that children in this era of globalization benefit positively from technology in the use of phones and other social media.

DESIRE TO ATTEND SPORTS AND ENTERTAINMENT SHOWS

Anyone who does not love or participate in sports and entertainment is questioned about their health because sports and entertainment are key indicators of a person's well-being. For children, it is even more crucial, as a healthy child is expected to be seen playing and enjoying leisure activities with their peers. This is the main reason why children cannot be separated from sports and entertainment.

According to psychological experts, Whitebread, Basilio, Kuvalja and Verma, sports have a significant relationship with the development of cognition and human emotions. These experts explain that this connection between sports and cognitive development contributes to the growth of language and other abilities that enable an individual to reach a level of self-sufficiency. They affirm that a child who does not engage in sports is not in a normal state of health and, conversely, sports have a significant role in building normal health for a child.[22] When a child is born and is still in the hands of doctors, the first sign they use to demonstrate the child's health is by playing with them in various ways. For that reason, I can say that sports are inherent to humans from birth.

Hence, considering the benefits of sports as outlined by psychologists, it is crucial for children to be given ample opportunities to engage in sports, as for some, sports reveal the talents they have been endowed with by God, which can be a part of their success capital in life. Indeed, children love to attend places where there are sports and entertainment.

21. Mjingwa, *Tamko la Roma*, para. 5.
22. Whitebread, Basilio, Kuvalja & Verma, *Importance of Play*, 31.

Therefore, parents and guardians should guide and protect children, especially when they want to attend and participate in sports and entertainment. In addition, parents should buy sports equipment for their children, such as balls, ropes, and cartoons, so that children have time to play even at home and do not feel the need to go to sports and entertainment venues, where they may expose themselves to unnecessary risks. Hence, since sports contribute to health, intelligence, talent, and employment, parents need to prioritize them for their children by providing careful supervision and monitoring.

DESIRE TO BUILD FRIENDSHIPS

The matter of relating in human life is a very good thing, and no mentally sound person can live without having relationships with fellow human beings. It is challenging to talk about building friendships without mentioning the concept of relationships. This concept of relationships can be interpreted in various ways. For example, Kazimoto explains that relationships are a psychological matter, involving the mind, thoughts, and emotions.[23]

On the other hand, Kivenule explains that the meaning of relationships is a state of closeness, neighborliness, friendship, unity, or cooperation that develops between relatives, family, or friends. Relationships involve being together mentally, physically, communicatively, spiritually, ideologically, developmentally, occupationally, socially, and in sports. These relationships are built on various foundations or ways, such as neighborliness, kinship, faith, ideology, work, and education.[24] Therefore, based on these perspectives as explained above, it is clear that friendship is built from relationships established between one person and another for various reasons, as outlined by Kivenule.

In simpler terms, I can say that friendship is a well-developed or grown relationship between two or more people. However,

23. Kazimoto, *Saikolojia ya Mahusiano*, para. 2.
24. Kivenule, *Mahusiano ya Wana Ndugu*, para. 1.

despite the reasons for relationships as explained above, all relationships have two sides, namely good and bad, or in other words, relationships or friendships are divided into two parts: good friendship and bad friendship.

Therefore, since any friendship starts off as good, it is challenging for children to foresee the end of their friendship as either good or bad when they start building friendships with each other as children. This is where parents and guardians should help their children understand how to build friendships from a young age to help them even when they become adults, knowing which friend is good for what purpose and which friend is bad for what purpose. Parents and guardians have the responsibility to teach their children the qualities of good and bad friends and the consequences arising from different styles of friendships. This emphasis aligns with the information provided by Mwanahiza that parents and guardians should deeply understand their children's friends.[25]

Examples of bad friends may have the following qualities: thieves, abusers, troublemakers, liars, disobedient to their parents in good matters, visitors, truants/disliking school, arrogant, disrespectful, and godless. In contrast, good qualities are the opposite of these, and children should be taught by parents and guardians, especially in these growing times of globalization. Therefore, I can say that if children are not helped to build good friendships, they may find themselves building bad friendships with their peers, considering that many children have been affected by significant moral decay resulting from poor upbringing, as explained in previous chapters of this book.

DESIRE TO ATTEND A GOOD SCHOOL

Recently, we have witnessed a significant awakening among parents and guardians in our community regarding the education of children, a result of the strong push from the government and education stakeholders with the goal of achieving the Millennium

---

25. Mwanahiza, *Utandawazi na Malezi*, para. 27.

Development Goals for education for all. Rugemalira affirms this awareness, stating that efforts have been made in the past five years through the primary education development program to improve primary schools to increase enrollment and achieve universal primary education (UPE).[26] This awareness has been fueled by the elimination of fees for primary and secondary schools in many countries, including Tanzania. This has generated a significant enthusiasm for attending school among many children at all levels.

However, due to this awareness, there has been a misconception among parents, guardians, and many children about the best schools for children. There is a belief that schools with an English curriculum, i.e., those using English as the language of instruction, are the best for a child. I consider this belief to be misguided because quality and the language of instruction are two different things. I believe that even schools with a Swahili curriculum as the official language of instruction can be excellent if their infrastructure and teaching environments are superior, as is the case with many schools that use English as the language of instruction.

One significant shortcoming of schools with an English curriculum, which is dangerous for the well-being of our culture, is that these schools, to a large extent, do not instill in children the upbringing that maintains our traditions and customs. Instead, children grow in an educational and ethical environment with a Western perspective. Rugemalira emphasizes that these schools are built on foundations that aim to strengthen the English language in schools to make children acquire the language using its natural environment. This is because many of these schools, using foreign languages such as English, French, etc., often employ foreign or local teachers who have lived abroad, and largely have experience in these languages, which are part of Western cultures.[27]

However, despite this shortcoming, many of these schools are good, and most of them have excellent environments and infrastructure to enable students to study and receive quality education, unlike many schools with a Swahili curriculum. Therefore,

---

26. Rugemalira, *Theoretical and Practical Challenges*, 67.
27. *Ibid*, 71.

parents and guardians who want to educate their children in these schools should ensure that their children do not stay in boarding but are day students. This way, they can continue to raise them in an environment that upholds the ethics of our society when they return home, so that they are not further affected by an upbringing with a Western orientation. This is because many children attending these schools still need close upbringing from their parents and guardians.

THE IMPORTANCE OF GLOBALIZATION

After thoroughly discussing the concept of globalization in various areas in this chapter and the previous chapters of this book, globalization seems to be viewed and interpreted by many people in our society as something bad, especially in matters of ethical upbringing and child development. In my view, I see the truth in this perspective only if we also consider the importance of globalization because I believe that everything has two sides, especially when we talk about goodness or badness. This means that everything that seems to have disadvantages also has its advantages, just as it is with globalization, which, despite having disadvantages, also has its importance.

Due to the growth of communication technology, leading to a significant increase in interactions among people from various cultures and the growth of people in a state of self-awareness and understanding of many analytical issues, which is the basis of globalization, it is clear that globalization has brought about some positive changes. For example, Trask in his explanation shows that globalization has helped expand job opportunities, families can strive for independence without relying heavily on the government in economic matters, health, and self-sufficiency in family security.[28] The issue of gender discrimination in various aspects of education and employment is also one of the significant changes in many societies worldwide due to the growth of globalization.

28. Trask, *Globalization and Families*, 3.

The United Nations' 2010 report shows a significant increase in employment for women within and outside their countries in different regions including Africa, Asia, Latin America and the Caribbean, and more developed regions as well.[29]

Apart from these successes as explained above, in many societies, especially in third-world countries like Tanzania, we have witnessed significant changes, especially in efforts to eliminate harmful traditions that are no longer suitable for the current society, such as female genital mutilation; limited opportunities for education, employment, leadership, and land ownership for women; killings of twins, albinos, and the elderly, etc. These issues, among others, show how we cannot ignore globalization starting from the family level and even the entire nation.

Therefore, based on the various explanations about the negative impacts of globalization along with its positives, I can say that on the other hand, globalization is very important, just like other things that have both good and bad sides. In simpler terms, taking a negative view of globalization would only make it worse, but taking a positive view would lead to positive results in families and society as a whole.

CONCLUSION

This chapter is crucial in this book, as well as the previous chapters, as it lays a strong foundation for understanding the concept of globalization. In this chapter, we see that globalization is not a new concept, as many people have described it, but rather a historical phenomenon. Furthermore, globalization is part of the family, and despite its weaknesses, there is no way for families to escape it; they must find ways to confront it. Also, in these times of globalization, children and young people largely live with emotions filled with various desires, and parents have a significant responsibility to help children control these desires.

29. United Nations, *The world's women 2010*, 86.

This chapter has shown that despite the apparent negativity in globalization, there is beauty within it. Therefore, it builds an understanding that, like other things, everything has both good and bad aspects, or vice versa.

QUESTIONS TO DISCUSS

(i) Globalization is not a new concept as commonly perceived, especially in third-world countries. Discuss with examples.

(ii) Everything that is visible to the naked eye or even through a microscope has both advantages and disadvantages. Discuss this statement in the context of the parenting aspect of globalization.

CHAPTER 7

Conclusion and Recommendations

IN THIS BOOK, THE issue of parenting has been thoroughly discussed from a broad perspective, focusing on the concept of globalization. The concept of globalization has been extensively explained to the point where counselors and advisors can teach the entire community to understand both the positive and negative aspects of globalization. This knowledge is essential for guiding child-rearing practices within the context of our society's traditions, customs, and culture. This is because globalization and its influence on the world today cannot be avoided in any way, even miraculously.

Parents, guardians, and the entire community need to understand that due to the rapid pace of scientific and technological development, we can no longer go back to the traditional way of life we lived in the past. Instead, we must move in tandem with these changes while carefully analyzing the positives and negatives that come with them.

To achieve the goal of effective parenting and building strong families in these times, it is crucial to recognize that families, defined as parents or guardians, cannot solely provide quality parenting and establish a strong family for the future of society and the nation as a whole. Instead, other institutions should take on the role of promoting quality parenting. Some of these institutions include:

i. Educational institutions such as schools and colleges, whose primary responsibility is to educate students on serving their communities with honesty, integrity, diligence, and patriotism while adhering to their cultural values. These institutions should use existing guidelines and policies to educate parents and children about the pros and cons of globalization and how to live in this era while respecting their good traditions. Technology should be used effectively to educate children.

ii. Religious institutions, including places of worship, whose major role is to preach good morals, integrity, and responsibility to their believers and the entire community. Faith should be used as a capital to help believers understand globalization in its good and bad aspects and how to live in a positive faith within this era. Religion should not be used to distort the truth about globalization and undermine upbringing and the generation that should face and confront globalization according to the will of the Almighty.

iii. Media outlets such as television, websites, newspapers, mobile phones, and various magazines should be utilized for parenting by providing teachings to the entire community through education, entertainment, and warnings via various programs shown on television such as news reports, drama series, productivity, the initiation of various projects, and good children's stories and classroom lessons.

iv. Government and its agencies such as parliament, the judiciary, the police, etc., should be accountable, especially in emphasizing and overseeing individuals, companies, and institutions that can cause a deterioration of morals in our society and especially for children. The issue of playing and distributing pornographic films and allowing some media outlets to publicly broadcast programs that do not align with the morals of our society is crucial; the government should enact regulatory laws. Moreover, the government, in collaboration with parents, should not allow actors in drama series to use very young children who have not mentally identified themselves in their performances. This should only be done under the special supervision of parents and especially in plays with good morals to help children develop their talents as good artists and future athletes.

In conclusion, the author provides an analogy about globalization that: "Globalization is like a bird flying overhead. The bird is meant to fly over our heads throughout its life, walking by flying over the heads of human beings who are smarter in analyzing good and bad than the bird itself, and we cannot stop it. Thus, it is the decision of a sane human being to allow or not to allow the bird to land on their head, build a nest, lay eggs, and then hatch chicks." The author welcomes counselors and advisors in family matters, social welfare professionals, and school teachers and lecturers to use this book as a valuable source of knowledge to help parents, guardians, and the community as a whole provide quality parenting for children in these times of globalization, which is like a turbulent sea whose waves, due to their speed, cannot be stopped by hands or cloth. The child is the parent and leader of the nation of tomorrow; it is essential to raise them well to achieve this perfection.

Bibliography

Achebe, Chinua. "The Trouble with Nigeria". Ibadan: Heinemann Educational Publishers, 1984.

Ashakiran, Deepthi R., and Deepthi. R. "Fast foods and their impact on health." *Journal of Krishna Institute of Medical Sciences University* 1, no. 2 (2012): 7–15.

Aye, Eucharia Nchedo, Immaculata Nwakaego Akaneme, Dorathy Ebere Adimora, Theresa O. Offorka, Amuda Robinson, Patience Okwudili Nwosu, and Felicia Ngozi Ekwealor. "Family Conflict and Managing Strategies: Implication for Understanding Emotion and Power Struggles." *Global Journal of Psychology Research: New Trends and Issues* 6, no. 3 (2016): 148–159.

Ayo, Millard. "Watoto Wafariki kwa Kuporomoka Ghorofa ya Kumi Wakati Mama Yao Akiwa Live Facebook." *Ayo TV*, September 14, 2021. Online at https://millardayo.com/watoto-wafariki-kwa-kuporomoka-ghorofa-ya-kumi-wakati-mama-yao-akiwa live facebook/ [Retrieved 14 September 2021].

Baraza la Kiswahili la Taifa [BAKITA] [The National Kiswahili Council]. *Kamusi Kuu ya Kiswahili (Toleo la 2)*. Dar es Salaam: Longhorn, 2017.

Baraza la Kiswahili la Zanzibar [BAKIZA] [The Council of Kiswahili Zanzibar]. *Kamusi ya Kiswahili Fasaha*. Nairobi: Oxford University Press, 2010.

Bejtkovský, Jiří. "Selected Current Trends in Human Resource Management in Health Service Providers in the Czech Republic." *Acta Universitatis Agriculturae et Silviculturae Mendelianae Brunensis* 65, no. 6 (2017): 1833–1840.

Bilqis, Nabilah. "Literature Review." 2019. Retrieved from http://repository.unpas.ac.id/46237/3/Chapter%20II.pdf. Accessed May 8, 2024.

British Broadcasting Corporation (BBC) News Swahili. "Smartphones zina athari gani kwa watoto?" 2014. Available at: https://www.bbc.com/swahili/habari/2014/02/140212_phones_watoto. Accessed on August 11, 2018.

Byrne, David. *Enabling Good Health for All. A reflection process for a new EU health strategy*. European Commission, 2004. Retrieved from: https://

ec.europa.eu/health/archive/ph_overview/documents/pub_good_health_en.pdf. Accessed on July 16, 2018.

Chama cha Wanasheria Tanzania Bara. *Mtoto na Haki Zake: Sheria katika Lugha Rahisi.* Dar es Salaam, 2016.

Chudhuri, Sumita. 2012. "Social Development and the Family." Accessed May 15, 2024. https://www.eolss.net/sample-chapters/c11/E1-11-02-04.pdf.

Commission for Human Security, CHS. *Human Security in Theory and Practice: Application of the Human Security Concept and the United Nations Trust Fund for Human Security.* New York: United Nations, 2009.

Deal, Terrence E., and Allan A. Kennedy. *Corporate Cultures: The Rites and Rituals of Corporate Life.* Reading, MA: Addison-Wesley, 1982.

Doughty, Julie, Lucy Reed KC, and Paul Magrath. *Transparency in the Family Courts: Publicity and Privacy in Practice.* 2nd ed. Sydney: Bloomsbury, 2024.

Duh, Mojca, and Jernej Belak. "Core Values, Culture and Ethical Climate in Family Versus Non-Family Enterprises." Paper presented at the MEB 2009-7th International Conference on Management, Enterprise and Benchmarking, Budapest, Hungary, June 5-6, 2009.

Fahey, Tony, Patricia Keilthy, and Ela Polek. *Family Relationships and Family Well-Being: A Study of the Families of Nine Year-Olds in Ireland.* University College Dublin and the Family Support Agency, 2012.

Gabriela, Vasciuc Să[set hacek over a]ndulescu Cristina. "The Necessity and Importance of Money in Time." *Ovidius University Annals, Economic Sciences Series* 18, no. 1 (2018): 417–21.

Gangel, Kenneth. *The Family First.* Minneapolis, MN: International Service, 1972.

Gilligan, Ian. "Clothing." In *Encyclopedia of Evolutionary Psychological Science,* edited by Todd K. Shackelford and Viviana A. Weekes-Shackelford, 2016. DOI 10.1007/978-3-319-16999-6_3009-1.

Grant, Ruth W., and Robert O. Keohane. "Accountability and Abuses of Power in World Politics." *The American Political Science Review* 99, no. 1 (February 2005): 29–43.

Guertin, Amy. "List of Family Values." Last modified May 8, 2024. Accessed May 8, 2024. https://www.lovetoknow.com/life/relationships/list-family-values.

Guest, David E. "HRM and Performance: Can Partnership Address the Dilemmas?" In *Human Resource Management: Ethics and Employment,* edited by Ashly H. Pinnington, Rob Macklin, and Tom Campbell. New York: Oxford University Press, 2007.

HAKIARDHI [The Land Rights Research & Resources Institute]. *Kijarida cha Kujielimisha juu ya Masuala Muhimu ya Ardhi, Mabadiliko ya Tabia Nchi, Utawala na Usimamizi wa Rasilimali Vijijini.* Vol. 1, 2017. http://ihi.kazi.pro/wordpress/wp-content/uploads/2017/10/content1.pdf. Accessed on September 1, 2018.

HakiElimu. *Elimu Bora ni Nini? Taarifa ya Utafiti kuhusu Mitazamo ya Wananchi na Stadi za Msingi za Watoto.* Dar es Salaam: HakiElimu, 2008.

Henggeler, Scott W., Sonja K. Schoenwald, Charles M. Borduin, Melisa D. Rowland, and Phillippe B. Cunningham. *Multi-systemic Treatment of Antisocial Behavior in Children and Adolescents.* New York: Guilford, 1998.

Huberts, Leo. W. J. C. "Integrity: What It Is and Why It Is Important." *Public Integrity* 0 (2018): 1–15. DOI: 10.1080/10999922.2018.1477404.

Hurtubise, Roch, Pierre-Olivier Babin, and Carolyne Grimard. "Understanding Shelters: An Overview of the Scientific Literature." 2007. Accessed May 11, 2024. https://homelesshub.ca/sites/default/files/Recension%20refuges%20final%20_version%20anglais_.pdf.

Hussein, Abdul Fattah Farea, and Yaser Hasan Salem Al-Mamary. "Conflicts: Their Types, and Their Negative and Positive Effects On Organizations." *International Journal of Scientific & Technology Research* 8, no. 8 (2019): 10–13.

Illinois Department of Children and Family Services [IDCFS]. *How to connect with your brothers and sisters: Information for youth, parents and caregivers.* 2014. Available at https://dcfs.illinois.gov/content/dam/soi/en/web/dcfs/documents/loving-homes/foster-care/documents/cfs_1050-95_sibling_visitation_rights_booklet.1.0.pdf. Accessed on May 16, 2024.

Jacobsen, Veronica, Lindy Fursman, John Bryant, Megan Claridge, and Benedikte Jensen. *Theories of the Family and Policy.* New Zealand Treasury Working Paper 04/02. Wellington, 2004.

Jamhuri ya Muungano wa Tanzania. *Katiba ya Jamhuri ya Muungano wa Tanzania ya Mwaka 1977.* Dar es Salaam, 1977.

Jamhuri ya Muungano wa Tanzania. *Sera ya Afya.* Dar es Salaam: Wizara ya Afya na Ustawi wa Jamii, 2007.

Johansson, Barbro. "Doing Age and Gender through Fashion." Paper from the Conference "INTER: A European Cultural Studies Conference in Sweden", organised by the Advanced Cultural Studies Institute of Sweden (ACSIS) in Norrköping 11–13 June 2007. Conference Proceedings published by Linköping University Electronic Press at www.ep.liu.se/ecp/025/.

Kazimoto, Elisha. "Saikolojia ya Mahusiano." 2016. https://materialadimu university2017.blogspot.com/2016/11/saikolojia-ya-mahusiano.html. Accessed on August 17, 2018.

Kenneth, Abban. "Understanding the Importance of Time Management to assistant Registrar's in the Registrars Department of the University of Education, Winneba." *International Journal of Scientific & Engineering Research* 3, no. 12 (2011): 1–16.

Kivenule, Adam Alphonce. "Mahusiano Baina ya Wana Ndugu Ndani ya Ukoo." 2013. http://adamkivenule.blogspot.com/2013/08/mahusiano-baina-ya-wanandugu-ndani-ya.html. Accessed on August 17, 2018.

Krone, Bob. "A Personal Philosophy." *Journal of Space Philosophy* 3, no. 2 (2014): 71–89.

Kumar, Suresh, and Sreeramana Aithal. "Time as a strategic resource in management of organizations." *ICTACT Journal on Management Studies* 6, no. 1(2020): 1138–1143. DOI: 10.21917/ijms.2020.0158

Li, Qiang, Anding Liu, Bin Li, Yixiao Li, Xianming Xu, and Hui Tao. "Research on the origin of clothing from the perspective of the ancient Chinese character etymology and philosophy." *Industria Textila* 72, no. 6 (2021): 651–58.

Madalina, Oachesu. "Conflict Management, a New Challenge." Paper presented at the 3rd Global Conference on Business, Economics, Management and Tourism, November 26–28, 2015, Rome, Italy. 2016.

Maina, Newton Kahumbi. *Muslim Education in Kenya with Special Reference to Madrasa System in Nairobi.* Unpublished M.A. Thesis, Kenyatta University, Nairobi. 1993.

Malunde, Kadama. "Migogoro ya ndoa chanzo cha uzururaji wa watoto, utoro na mimba za utotoni msalala." 2021. Retrieved from https://shinyangapress.blogspot.com/2021/09/migogoro-ya-ndoa-chanzo-cha-uzururaji.html. Accessed on November 8, 2021.

Masare, Alawi. "How Billions in Unclaimed Money Goes Unchecked." *The Citizen*, April 18, 2021. Accessed November 5, 2021. https://www.thecitizen.co.tz/tanzania/news/how-billions-in-unclaimed-money-goes-unchecked-3367030.

Mattaini, Mark A. *Clinical Intervention with Families.* Washington, DC: NASW, 1999.

Mbonde, John P. "Methali za Kiutandawazi." Paper presented at the Jubilee Conference of 75 Years of TUKI, University of Dar es Salaam, July 4–7, 2005.

Mjigwa, Richard A. "Papa Francisko Sakramenti ya Mpako wa Wagonjwa: Upendo na Faraja." 2021. Retrieved from https://www.vaticannews.va/sw/pope/news/2021-07/papa-francisko-sakramenti-mpako-wagonjwa-huduma-upendo-faraja.html. Accessed on November 9, 2021.

Mjigwa, Richard A. "Tamko la Roma: Ulinzi wa utu na heshima ya watoto wadogo." 2017. Retrieved from http://www.archivioradiovaticana.va/storico/2017/10/07/tamko_la_roma_ulinzi_wa_utu_na_heshima_ya_watoto_wadogo!/sw-1341560. Accessed on May 11, 2021.

Mlaga, Wallace. "Euphrase Kezilahabi kama Mwanafalsafa Kamili: Mifano Kutoka Riwaya ya Mzingile." *MULIKA* 37 (2019): 1–22.

Mohamed, M. A., and Mohamed, S. A. *Kamusi ya Visawe: Swahili Dictionary Synonyms.* Dar es Salaam: East African Educational, 2008.

Mohtar, Shahimi, and Mazhar Abbas. "Teenager's Preferences and Choice Behavior towards Branded or Unbranded Products." *Journal of Business and Management* 16, no. 7 (2014): 98–103.

Mrikaria, Steven Elisamia. "Fasihi Simulizi na Teknolojia Mpya." *Swahili Forum* 14 (2007):197-206. Available at: https://ul.qucosa.de/api/qucosa%3A11795/attachment/ATT-0/. Accessed on May 15, 2024.

Mwanahiza, Mdee. "Utandawazi na Malezi." Last modified June 27, 2011. Accessed August 17, 2018. http://wajengadunia.blogspot.com/2011/06/utandawazi-na-malezi.html.

Mwangosi, Gerephace. "Riwaya ya Babu Alipofufuka na Utandawazi Nchini Tanzania." *Ruaha Journal of Arts and Social Sciences* 4 (2018): 123–36.

Newman, Leanne Lewis. "Faith, Spirituality, and Religion: A Model for Understanding the Differences." 2004. Available at https://files.eric.ed.gov/fulltext/EJ956981.pdf. Accessed May 10, 2024.

Ngugi, Pamela M.Y. "Fasihi ya Wototo katika Kutekeleza Mahitaji ya Mtoto Kisaikolojia." 2017. Retrieved from http://journals.udsm.ac.tz/index.php/kiswahili/article/download/1024/953. Accessed on August 8, 2018.

Nickell, Paulena, and Jean Muir Dorsey. *Management in Family Living*. 4th ed. New York: John Wiley & Sons, 1967.

———. *Management in Family Living*. 3rd ed. New York: John Wiley & Sons, 1959.

Nincic, Miroslav, and Jennifer M. Ramos. "The Dynamics of Patriotism: Survey and Experimental Evidence." 2009. Paper presented at the annual meeting of the American Political Science Association, Toronto. Available at SSRN: https://ssrn.com/abstract=1450500.

Njau, Mary, Alphonce Katemi, Athanasia Soka, and Scholastica Jullu. *Haki za Mwanamke Katika Sheria za Ardhi*. Dar es Salaam: Kituo cha Msaada wa Sheria kwa Wanawake (WLAC), 2013.

Oladipo, Olowookere Peter. "Forms and Functions of Traditional Dress." *Journal of Resourcefulness and Distinction* 12, no. 1 (2016): 69–83.

Perkins, Kelsey Evelyn. "The Integrated Model of Self-Confidence: Defining and Operationalizing Self-Confidence in Organizational Settings." Unpublished Doctorate of Philosophy in Industrial/Organizational Psychology, University of Melbourne, Florida. 2018.

Rajan, Sonika. "Process of Social Change." 2020. Available at https://itcollege.ac.in/itdc/wp-content/uploads/2020/10/Dr-Sonika-Rajan-3.pdf. Accessed on May 15, 2024.

Rotilă, Viorel. "The Relationship Between Religion and Society from the Evolutionary Perspective; the 'Evolutionary Wager of Religion.'" *International Multidisciplinary Scientific Conference on the Dialogue between Sciences & Arts, Religion & Education* 3 (2019): 122–31. DOI: 10.26520/mcdsare.2019.3.122-131.

Rugemalira, Josephat M. "Theoretical and Practical Challenges in a Tanzanian English Medium Primary School." *Africa & Asia* 5 (2005): 66–84.

Rwegelera, Martina K. "The effect of globalization on Tanzanian culture: A review." *Huria Journal of the Open University of Tanzania* 12, no. 1 (2012): 152–72.

Smalley, Gary. *The Key to Your Child's Heart*. Edited by Jonathan Menn. Translated by Michael D. Nyangusi. Appleton, WI: Equipping Church Leaders East Africa, 2008-2013.

Spellings, Margaret. Foreword. In: *Helping Your Child Become a Responsible Citizen*. Washington, D.C: U. S. Department of Education, 2005.

Thakore, Digvijaysinh. "Conflict and Conflict Management." *Journal of Business and Management* 8, no. 6 (2013): 07–16.

Toussaint, Eric. *Globalization from Christopher Columbus, Vasco da Gama and Ferdinand Magellan until Today*. 2021. Available at https://www.cadtm. org/Globalization-from-Christopher-Columbus-Vasco-da-Gama-and-Ferdinand-Magellan-20487. Accessed May 15, 2024.

Trask, Bahira Sherif. *Globalization and Families: Meeting the Family Policy Challenge*. University of Delaware, 2011. Retrieved from: http://www. un.org/esa/socdev/family/docs/egm11/Traskpaper.pdf. Accessed on August 17, 2018.

United Nations Children's Fund [UNICEF]. *Defining Quality in Education*. New York, NY: UNICEF, 2000.

United Nations Development Programme. "Arab Knowledge Report 2010/2011. General Report: Social Upbringing and Preparation for the Knowledge Society." Accessed May 15, 2024. https://www.undp.org/sites/g/files/ zskgke326/files/migration/arabstates/AKR2010-2011-Eng-Chapter3.pdf.

United Nations World Tourism Organization [UNWTO]. *Understanding tourism: Basic Glossary*. 2008. Retrieved from https://webunwto.s3-eu-west-1.amazonaws.com/2019-08/glossary_EN.pdf. Accessed on August 10, 2018.

United Nations. *The World's Women 2010: Trends and Statistics*. New York, NY: Department of Economic and Social Affairs, 2010.

University of York. "Financial resources: What are they and how are they managed?" 2022. Available at https://online.york.ac.uk/financial-resources-what-are-they-and-how-are-they-managed/. Accessed on May 15, 2024.

Uwe, E. A., Patrick N. Asuquo, and Emmanuel Etta Ekuri. "Parenting and Responsibility: Holding Parents Accountable for Children's Antisocial Practices." *Journal of Human Ecology* 24, no. 1 (2008): 51–57.

Whitebread, David, Marisol Basilio, Martina Kuvalja, and Mohini Verma. *The importance of play. A report on the value of children's play with a series of policy recommendations*. Written for Toy Industries of Europe (TIE) April 2012. University of Cambridge. 2012. Available at: https://www.csap.cam. ac.uk/media/uploads/files/1/david-whitebread---importance-of-play-report.pdf. Accessed on May 16, 2024.

World Health Organization [WHO]. *Constitution of the World Health Organization*.1948. Retrieved from: https://www.loc.gov/law/help/us-treaties/bevans/m-ust000004-0119.pdf. Accessed on July 16, 2018.

Zlotin, Boris, and Alla Zusman. *The Concept of Resources in TRIZ: Past, Present and Future*. Southfield, Michigan: Ideation International, 2005.

Zombwe, Mtemi Gervas. "Manufaa ya Kudumisha Haki za Watoto: Kuheshimu Haki za Watoto ni Kujenga Taifa lenye Haki na Amani." *HakiElimu Working Papers*. Dar Es Salaam, 2010.